Cocktail Pa

BUSINESS AND
GENERAL
REFERENCE
BOOK SERIES
FROM IDG

Sheet

D0376346

Quick Cocktail Music Guide

Style of Music	Typical Artist(s)
Space age bachelor pad	Juan Garcia Esquivel
Exotica	Yma Sumach, Les Baxter, Martin Denny, Arthur Lyman
Latin music	Joao Gilberto, Sergio Mendez and Brazil '66
Lounge	Joey Altruda, Mike Flowers Pops
Big band swing	Frank Sinatra, Duke Ellington
Surf	The Ventures, Dick Dale, Shadowy Men from a Shadowy Planet
Muzak	Montovanni, Jackie Gleason Orchestra, Ray Conniff Singers, Percy Faith
Movie soundtracks	Look for the movie title, but film scores featuring songs by Burt Bacharach or Henry Mancini go over well at parties

How to Make a Martini

Ingredients

2 oz.   Vodka or gin

Dash   Extra dry vermouth

Directions

Shake or stir vodka or gin and vermouth over ice. Strain and serve in a cocktail glass straight up or over ice. Garnish with a twist or an olive.

...For Dummies: Bestselling Book Series for Beginners

Cocktail Parties For Dummies™

Cheat Sheet

Checklist for the Day of the Party

- ✔ Prepare the food as early in the day as possible.

- ✔ If the party's not at home, go to the venue and put up your decorations right after preparing the food.

- ✔ Set up the bar — get liquor and mixers, cool the beer, cut and prepare the garnishes, pick up equipment.

- ✔ Test your audio system and lighting.

- ✔ Put out your flowers.

- ✔ Freshen up your bathroom by putting out clean towels, fresh soap, and tissues, and make sure that nothing is in the bathroom that you don't want someone to see.

- ✔ Walk through your party area with trouble in mind. Fix any problems.

- ✔ Have your hair done and get your nails manicured.

How Much Liquor Will You Need?

If You're Entertaining	Pre-Dinner Cocktails You'll Average	For a Party You'll Average
4 People	8 to 12 Drinks	12 to 16 Drinks
6 People	12 to 18 Drinks	18 to 24 Drinks
8 People	16 to 24 Drinks	24 to 32 Drinks
12 People	24 to 36 Drinks	36 to 48 Drinks
20 People	40 to 60 Drinks	60 to 80 Drinks
25 People	50 to 70 Drinks	75 to 100 Drinks
40 People	80 to 120 Drinks	120 to 160 Drinks

IDG BOOKS WORLDWIDE™

...For Dummies: Bestselling Book Series for Beginners

Praise for Cocktail Parties For Dummies

"*Cocktail Parties For Dummies* is an invaluable how-to, a spunky, practical guide that's a party in itself."

— Michael Musto, *Village Voice* Columnist

"If you want to throw a party, be the life of the party, or BE a party, there's no better expert than Jaymz Bee. Here's a book that tells it all! Setting, music, how to dress, and best of all, how to carry off a swinger's attitude that will have you looking like a founding member of the Rat Pack!"

— Mark Breslin, Chief Executive Officer, Yuk Yuk's International

"From venues to menus, from party themes to party schemes, this delightful read has it all!!"

— Barbara Hershenhorn, President, Party Barbara Co.

"*Cocktail Parties For Dummies* is a curious blend of Canadian Club and Canadian humor for the party-goer/giver."

— Joseph Lanza, author of *The Cocktail: The Influence of Spirits on the American Psyche*

"*Cocktail Parties For Dummies* will make any cad gathering a truly swingin' affair."

— Sam Wick, *Lounge Magazine*

"Whether you're a polished hostess or planning your first party, this book will have your guests happily sitting, standing, sipping, munching, and mingling. And where will you be? Right in there with them, being fabulous, doing the party thing, according to Jaymz Bee. People scramble to get to his parties — now the world knows why.

— Sara Waxman, Chair, Gold and Silver Anniversary Opera Ball

"'A merry heart doeth good like a medicine,' says the proverb, and this is one heck of a merry book and Jaymz Bee is a very merry fellar."

— Alan Dunn, Logistics Director, Rolling Stones World Tour '97/'98

COCKTAIL PARTIES FOR DUMMIES™

by Jaymz Bee

with Jan Gregor

IDG Books Worldwide, Inc.
An International Data Group Company

Foster City, CA ♦ Chicago, IL ♦ Indianapolis, IN ♦ Southlake, TX

Cocktail Parties For Dummies™

Published by
IDG Books Worldwide, Inc.
An International Data Group Company
919 E. Hillsdale Blvd.
Suite 400
Foster City, CA 94404
www.idgbooks.com (IDG Books Worldwide Web site)
www.dummies.com (Dummies Press Web site)

Library of Congress Catalog Card No.: 97-80183

ISBN: 0-7645-5026-8

Printed in the United States of America

10 9 8 7 6 5 4 3 2 1

1P/RV/QZ/ZX/IN

Distributed in the United States by IDG Books Worldwide, Inc.

Distributed by Macmillan Canada for Canada; by Transworld Publishers Limited in the United Kingdom; by IDG Norge Books for Norway; by IDG Sweden Books for Sweden; by Woodslane Pty. Ltd. for Australia; by Woodslane Enterprises Ltd. for New Zealand; by Longman Singapore Publishers Ltd. for Singapore, Malaysia, Thailand, and Indonesia; by Simron Pty. Ltd. for South Africa; by Toppan Company Ltd. for Japan; by Distribuidora Cuspide for Argentina; by Livraria Cultura for Brazil; by Ediciencia S.A. for Ecuador; by Addison-Wesley Publishing Company for Korea; by Ediciones ZETA S.C.R. Ltda. for Peru; by WS Computer Publishing Corporation, Inc., for the Philippines; by Unalis Corporation for Taiwan; by Contemporanea de Ediciones for Venezuela; by Computer Book & Magazine Store for Puerto Rico; by Express Computer Distributors for the Caribbean and West Indies. Authorized Sales Agent: Anthony Rudkin Associates for the Middle East and North Africa.

For general information on IDG Books Worldwide's books in the U.S., please call our Consumer Customer Service department at 800-762-2974. For reseller information, including discounts and premium sales, please call our Reseller Customer Service department at 800-434-3422.

For information on where to purchase IDG Books Worldwide's books outside the U.S., please contact our International Sales department at 415-655-3200 or fax 415-655-3295.

For information on foreign language translations, please contact our Foreign & Subsidiary Rights department at 415-655-3021 or fax 415-655-3281.

For sales inquiries and special prices for bulk quantities, please contact our Sales department at 415-655-3200 or write to the address above.

For information on using IDG Books Worldwide's books in the classroom or for ordering examination copies, please contact our Educational Sales department at 800-434-2086 or fax 817-251-8174.

For press review copies, author interviews, or other publicity information, please contact our Public Relations department at 415-655-3000 or fax 415-655-3299.

For authorization to photocopy items for corporate, personal, or educational use, please contact Copyright Clearance Center, 222 Rosewood Drive, Danvers, MA 01923, or fax 508-750-4470.

is a trademark under exclusive
license to IDG Books Worldwide, Inc.,
from International Data Group, Inc.

About the Authors

Jaymz Bee, the "King of Cocktail," is at the center of a sound and scene that is reclaiming the word "party" and making it, well, civilized.

In sync with a worldwide "revolt into style," Jaymz is not so much jumping on a bandwagon as he is welcoming the world aboard the bandwagon he's been driving since he was born in the middle of the swinging '60s in Canada.

A family vacation to Las Vegas when Jaymz was only 16 made a profound and lasting impression on him: "I wasn't thinking about gamblers losing their children's college tuition. All I could see was colorful drinks, hilarious fashion, and bright lights. As soon as I got home, I bought a baby-blue polyester safari suit."

Jaymz spent the 1980s establishing himself in the music industry, touring extensively through Europe and Canada as the front man/singer for the group Look People. In Toronto he landed the job as musical director on *Friday Night,* a weekly variety/talk show on the CBC.

While in Toronto, Jaymz began his career as a party consultant. He has thrown parties for both celebrity and corporate events. His clients have included filmmaker Wes Craven, "Weird Al" Yankovic, Tom Hanks, Jim Carrey, and the late LSD/cyberspace guru Timothy Leary.

In 1996, Jaymz caught the attention of BMG Music Canada President Paul Alofs (a cocktail aficionado), who hired Jaymz as a consultant and then made him president of a newly formed record label to bring cocktail music to the masses. Jaymz named the label Leisure Lab, a reference to his devotion to the art of living in style.

Jaymz and his band, The Royal Jelly Orchestra, have a series of successful releases available worldwide on the Milan/BMG label, including *Cocktail: Shakin' and Stirred* and *A Christmas Cocktail.*

One thing Bee wants to make very clear: This party is for everyone!

* * *

Jan Gregor is a Seattle-based freelance writer who has worked in the entertainment business for more than 20 years, including hosting private parties and catering for large touring shows. He managed a sideshow troupe's around-the-world tour and recently authored a narrative nonfiction book on that experience. He met Jaymz Bee in Eastern Canada in 1992.

ABOUT IDG BOOKS WORLDWIDE

Welcome to the world of IDG Books Worldwide.

IDG Books Worldwide, Inc., is a subsidiary of International Data Group, the world's largest publisher of computer-related information and the leading global provider of information services on information technology. IDG was founded more than 25 years ago and now employs more than 8,500 people worldwide. IDG publishes more than 275 computer publications in over 75 countries (see listing below). More than 60 million people read one or more IDG publications each month.

Launched in 1990, IDG Books Worldwide is today the #1 publisher of best-selling computer books in the United States. We are proud to have received eight awards from the Computer Press Association in recognition of editorial excellence and three from Computer Currents' First Annual Readers' Choice Awards. Our best-selling ...For Dummies® series has more than 30 million copies in print with translations in 30 languages. IDG Books Worldwide, through a joint venture with IDG's Hi-Tech Beijing, became the first U.S. publisher to publish a computer book in the People's Republic of China. In record time, IDG Books Worldwide has become the first choice for millions of readers around the world who want to learn how to better manage their businesses.

Our mission is simple: Every one of our books is designed to bring extra value and skill-building instructions to the reader. Our books are written by experts who understand and care about our readers. The knowledge base of our editorial staff comes from years of experience in publishing, education, and journalism — experience we use to produce books for the '90s. In short, we care about books, so we attract the best people. We devote special attention to details such as audience, interior design, use of icons, and illustrations. And because we use an efficient process of authoring, editing, and desktop publishing our books electronically, we can spend more time ensuring superior content and spend less time on the technicalities of making books.

You can count on our commitment to deliver high-quality books at competitive prices on topics you want to read about. At IDG Books Worldwide, we continue in the IDG tradition of delivering quality for more than 25 years. You'll find no better book on a subject than one from IDG Books Worldwide.

John Kilcullen
CEO
IDG Books Worldwide, Inc.

Steven Berkowitz
President and Publisher
IDG Books Worldwide, Inc.

 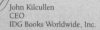

Eighth Annual
Computer Press
Awards ≥1992

Ninth Annual
Computer Press
Awards ≥1993

Tenth Annual
Computer Press
Awards ≥1994

Eleventh Annual
Computer Press
Awards ≥1995

IDG Books Worldwide, Inc., is a subsidiary of International Data Group, the world's largest publisher of computer-related information and the leading global provider of information services on information technology. International Data Group publishes over 275 computer publications in over 75 countries. Sixty million people read one or more International Data Group publications each month. International Data Group's publications include: ARGENTINA: Buyer's Guide, Computerworld Argentina, PC World Argentina; AUSTRALIA: Australian Macworld, Australian PC World, Australian Reseller News, Computerworld, IT Casebook, Network World, Publish, Webmaster; AUSTRIA: Computerwelt Osterreich, Networks Austria, PC Tip Austria; BANGLADESH: PC World Bangladesh; BELARUS: PC World Belarus; BELGIUM: Data News; BRAZIL: Annuário de Informática, Computerworld, Connections, Macworld, PC Player, PC World, Publish, Reseller News, Supergamepower; BULGARIA: Computerworld Bulgaria, Network World Bulgaria, PC & MacWorld Bulgaria; CANADA: CIO Canada, Client/Server World, ComputerWorld Canada, InfoWorld Canada, NetworkWorld Canada, WebWorld; CHILE: Computerworld Chile, PC World Chile; COLOMBIA: Computerworld Colombia, PC World Colombia; COSTA RICA: PC World Centro America; THE CZECH AND SLOVAK REPUBLICS: Computerworld Czechoslovakia, Macworld Czech Republic, PC World Czechoslovakia; DENMARK: Communications World Danmark, Computerworld Danmark, Macworld Danmark, PC World Danmark, Techworld Denmark; DOMINICAN REPUBLIC: PC World Republica Dominicana; ECUADOR: PC World Ecuador; EGYPT: Computerworld Middle East, PC World Middle East; EL SALVADOR: PC World Centro America; FINLAND: MikroPC, Tietoverkko, Tietoviikko; FRANCE: Distributique, Hebdo, Info PC, Le Monde Informatique, Macworld, Reseaux & Telecoms, WebMaster France; GERMANY: Computer Partner, Computerwoche, Computerwoche Extra, Computerwoche FOCUS, Global Online, Macwelt, PC Welt; GREECE: Amiga Computing, GamePro Greece, Multimedia World; GUATEMALA: PC World Centro America; HONDURAS: PC World Centro America; HONG KONG: Computerworld Hong Kong, PC World Hong Kong, Publish in Asia; HUNGARY: ABCD CD-ROM, Computerworld Szamitastechnika, Internetto online Magazine, PC World Hungary, PC-X Magazin Hungary; ICELAND: Tolvuheimur PC World Island; INDIA: Information Communications World, Information Systems Computerworld, PC World India, Publish in Asia; INDONESIA: InfoKomputer PC World, Komputek Computerworld, Publish in Asia; IRELAND: ComputerScope, PC Live!; ISRAEL: Macworld Israel, People & Computers/Computerworld; ITALY: Computerworld Italia, Macworld Italia, Networking Italia, PC World Italia; JAPAN: DTP World, Macworld Japan, Nikkei Personal Computing, OS/2 World Japan, SunWorld Japan, Windows NT World, Windows World Japan; KENYA: PC World East African; KOREA: Hi-Tech Information, Macworld Korea, PC World Korea; MACEDONIA: PC World Macedonia; MALAYSIA: Computerworld Malaysia, PC World Malaysia, Publish in Asia; MALTA: PC World Malta; MEXICO: Computerworld Mexico, PC World Mexico; MYANMAR: PC World Myanmar; NETHERLANDS: Computer! Totaal, LAN Internetworking Magazine, LAN World Buyers Guide, Macworld Netherlands, Net, WebWereld; NEW ZEALAND: Absolute Beginners Guide and Plain & Simple Series, Computer Buyer, Computer Industry Directory, Computerworld New Zealand, MTB, Network World, PC World New Zealand; NICARAGUA: PC World Centro America; NORWAY: Computerworld Norge, CW Rapport, Datamagasinet, Financial Rapport, Kursguide Norge, Macworld Norge, Multimediaworld Norge, PC World Ekspress Norge, PC World Nettverk, PC World Norge, PC World ProduktGuide Norge; PAKISTAN: Computerworld Pakistan; PANAMA: PC World Panama; PEOPLE'S REPUBLIC OF CHINA: China Computer Users, China Computerworld, China InfoWorld, China Telecom World Weekly, Computer & Communication, Electronic Design China, Electronics Today, Electronics Weekly, Game Software, PC World China, Popular Computer Week, Software Weekly, Software World, Telecom World; PERU: Computerworld Peru, PC World Profesional Peru, PC World SoHo Peru; PHILIPPINES: Click!, Computerworld Philippines, PC World Philippines, Publish in Asia; POLAND: Computerworld Poland, Computerworld Special Report Poland, Cyber, Macworld Poland, Networld Poland, PC World Komputer; PORTUGAL: Cerebro/PC World, Computerworld/Correio Informático, Dealer World Portugal, Mac*In/PC*In Portugal, Multimedia World; PUERTO RICO: PC World Puerto Rico; ROMANIA: Computerworld Romania, PC World Romania, Telecom Romania; RUSSIA: Computerworld Russia, Mir PK, Publish, Seti; SINGAPORE: Computerworld Singapore, PC World Singapore, Publish in Asia; SLOVENIA: Monitor; SOUTH AFRICA: Computing SA, Network World SA, Software World SA; SPAIN: Communicaciones World España, Computerworld España, Dealer World España, Macworld España, PC World España; SRI LANKA: Infolink PC World; SWEDEN: CAP&Design, Computer Sweden, Corporate Computing Sweden, Internetworld Sweden, it.branschen, Macworld Sweden, MaxiData Sweden, MikroDatorn, Nätverk & Kommunikation, PC World Sweden, PCaktiv, Windows World Sweden; SWITZERLAND: Computerworld Schweiz, Macworld Schweiz, PCtip; TAIWAN: Computerworld Taiwan, Macworld Taiwan, NEW ViSION/Publish, PC World Taiwan, Windows World Taiwan; THAILAND: PC World in Asia, Thai Computerworld; TURKEY: Computerworld Turkiye, Macworld Turkiye, Network World Turkiye, PC World Turkiye; UKRAINE: Computerworld Kiev, Multimedia World Ukraine, PC World Ukraine; UNITED KINGDOM: Acorn User UK, Amiga Action UK, Amiga Computing UK, Apple Talk UK, Computing, Macworld, Parents and Computers UK, PC Advisor, PC Home, PSX Pro, The WEB; UNITED STATES: Cable in the Classroom, CIO Magazine, Computerworld, DOS World, Federal Computer Week, GamePro Magazine, InfoWorld, I-Way, Macworld, Network World, PC Games, PC World, Publish, Video Event, THE WEB Magazine, and WebMaster; online webzines: JavaWorld, NetscapeWorld, and SunWorld Online; URUGUAY: InfoWorld Uruguay; VENEZUELA: Computerworld Venezuela, PC World Venezuela; and VIETNAM: PC World Vietnam.
3/24/97

Dedication

This book is dedicated to Laura Kikauka and Gordon Monahon, a cocktail couple extraordinaire! They treat all guests like royalty and have thrown many of the greatest cocktail theme parties I've ever attended.

Jaymz Bee's Acknowledgments

This book couldn't have happened without Jan Gregor, a friend in Seattle who helped with some of the writing and helped provide ideas. I'd also like to thank Joe Kilmartin and Paul Myers for their research work, written contributions, and their personal support, and Brian Ainsworth, who manages the party that is my life.

Credits for the photo team include:

Photography: Graham Kennedy

Models: Dana Dynamite, Josielynne Evidente, Justina Ferro, Lori Lofchick, Melleny Melody, Marika Samitz, Rebecca Vile

Hair and makeup: Lori Lofchick

Stylist: Rebecca Vile

Thank you to Kurt Swinghammer for the caricature of me that served as the basis for the Jaymz Sayz icon. Finally, a round of drinks for:

Mark Collis	Mimi	Kelly Cornell
Great Bob Scott	Norm Gauthier	Del Greger
Jamie Grant	Jono Grant	Bazl Salazar
Robert Shuttleworth	Christine Gaffney	Maire Devine
Sir Spinner Fine Vinyl	Chris Lang	Xtina King
Georgia Villeneuve	Rickio Woods	Doug Zangar
Linda Derschang	John Sutton	Clive Smith
Glenn Smith	Joanne Smale	Liza Algar
Denise Donlon	Joel Goldberg	Jefferson T. Miles
John Kilcullen	Rev Mengle	Tammy Castleman

Publisher's Acknowledgments

We're proud of this book; please send us your comments about it by using the
IDG Books Worldwide Registration Card at the back of the book or by e-mailing
us at feedback/dummies@idgbooks.com. Some of the people who helped bring
this book to market include the following:

Acquisitions, Development, and Editorial

Project Editor: Rev Mengle

Acquisitions Editor: Sarah Kennedy, Executive Editor

Senior Copy Editor: Tamara Castleman

Editorial Manager: Colleen Rainsberger

Editorial Assistant: Donna Love

Production

Project Coordinator: Regina Snyder

Layout and Graphics: J. Tyler Conner, Angela F, Hunckler, Jane E. Martin, Drew R. Moore, Heather N. Pearson, Brent Savage, Kate Snell, Michael A. Sullivan

Proofreaders: Laura L. Bowman, Michelle Croninger, Joel K. Draper, Janet M. Withers, Karen York

Indexer: Liz Cunningham

Special Help

Stephanie Koutek, Proof Editor; Ann Miller, Editorial Coordinator; Nickole J. Harris, Acquisitions Coordinator; Jill Alexander, Acquisitions Assistant.

General and Administrative

IDG Books Worldwide, Inc.: John Kilcullen, CEO; Steven Berkowitz, President and Publisher

IDG Books Technology Publishing: Brenda McLaughlin, Senior Vice President and Group Publisher

Dummies Technology Press and Dummies Editorial: Diane Graves Steele, Vice President and Associate Publisher; Kristin A. Cocks, Editorial Director; Mary Bednarek, Acquisitions and Product Development Director

Dummies Trade Press: Kathleen A. Welton, Vice President and Publisher

IDG Books Production for Dummies Press: Beth Jenkins, Production Director; Cindy L. Phipps, Manager of Project Coordination, Production Proofreading, and Indexing; Kathie S. Schutte, Supervisor of Page Layout; Shelley Lea, Supervisor of Graphics and Design; Debbie J. Gates, Production Systems Specialist; Robert Springer, Supervisor of Proofreading; Debbie Stailey, Special Projects Coordinator; Tony Augsburger, Supervisor of Reprints and Bluelines; Leslie Popplewell, Media Archive Coordinator

Dummies Packaging and Book Design: Patti Sandez, Packaging Specialist; Lance Kayser, Packaging Assistant; Kavish + Kavish, Cover Design

♦

The publisher would like to give special thanks to Patrick J. McGovern, without whom this book would not have been possible.

♦

Contents at a Glance

Cartoons at a Glance

By Rich Tennant

page 207

page 79

page 189

page 5

page 131

page 37

Fax: 508-546-7747 • E-mail: the5wave@tiac.net

Table of Contents

Introduction

Some people visit Switzerland to find inspiration among the Alps. I was just there working on my entertainment career when I found a kind of calling.

During the summer of 1988, I was based in Zurich with my drummer and best friend, Great Bob Scott. Bob and I were doing our usual impromptu street performance art — poetry, percussion, and puppets — when we were asked by a man named Ueli Steinle to perform at a party for some rich and influential Swiss. My parents and their friends really knew how to live, so I'd been to several cocktail parties at an early age, but I wasn't prepared for Mr. Steinle's spectacle.

Ueli rented a warehouse on Lake Zurich and filled it with exotic plants and large dining tables, with a huge stage at one end and a comfortable bar at the other. The evening began with people being greeted at the door by beautiful Brazilian women and the host. Security wore tuxedos and the waiters and waitresses were dressed in typical black and white "French service" outfits.

Mr. Steinle also hired several performers, the best street performers in town. Although Great Bob and I were only to have played a very small part in that event (performing before the dessert), we ended up doing a comical a cappella version of "Bohemian Rhapsody" by the cocktail bar in the wee hours.

In short, the cocktail party was elegant, it was fun, and it was inspiring — so inspiring that it motivated me to return to Toronto and throw ginormous (that's gigantic and enormous) cocktail parties of my own. Through my various projects (particularly the musical group, Look People), I met movers and shakers who attended my parties and began to spread the word. Before I knew it, I was asked to run a nightclub (The Beehive), and I began doing film wrap and record release parties. Hundreds of parties later, I still enjoy the planning and pleasure every party brings.

Do You Want to Party?

Great! This book shows you how to party the cocktail way. I make no assumptions as to the experience of my readers. People looking to throw their first party will find everything explained clearly. Experienced party hosts can benefit from some of the ideas and tips I provide.

Does that mean you should read this book from front to back? Not necessarily. The chapters are designed to tell you everything you need to know about a given topic, or let you know where else in the book relevant information is discussed, so you can start anywhere that interests you. Can you still read the book from front to back? Sure. Go ahead. See if I care!

How This Book Is Organized

This book is divided into parts, and each part is divided into chapters. Here's what each part is about.

Part I: Basic Considerations

You can, of course, throw a cocktail party anytime and invite anyone you want. But really memorable cocktail parties require some attention to detail. Do you want a big party or a small party? Where are you going to have it? Who are you going to invite? When are you going to have it? This part guides you through these crucial early decisions.

Part II: The Theme's the Thing

The stereotypical cocktail party is an elegant affair, with men in tuxedoes and ladies in nice dresses. Certainly, that's one cocktail party idea — but not the only one. Ever been to a Rubik's Cube party? What about a Spy bash? Turn to this section for ideas for large and small parties, and learn how to let your cocktail-party-planning imagination run wild.

Part III: Setting the Mood

Parties don't just happen — they take a little effort. From guests' first look at your invitation to the decorations on your walls and floors to the music playing softly in the background, you want everything about your event to put your guests in the party mood. This part has suggestions on invitations, decorating, and music to make your party stand out.

Part IV: Drinks and Food

Unlike some parties, a cocktail party isn't all about food and drink — but you certainly can't ignore them. This part has both drink recipes and hors d'oeuvre recipes to help you decide what you want to serve, how you want to serve it, and how much you're going to need.

Part V: Doing the Party Thing

Okay, you have the date, you have the theme, and you have a general idea of what else to do, but what should be the first thing on your list? This part explains what to do when, both in the weeks before the party and as the guests are arriving. You'll also find some tips on how to handle mishaps and misfits, to keep those unexpected happenings from ruining your party.

Part VI: The Part of Tens

People who love lists will love this part, which includes do's and don'ts for cocktail party guests, essential cocktail party Web sites, films to put you in the cocktail mood, and my list of heroes in the cocktail movement.

In the back is an appendix that expands on the music chapter with a listing of cocktail party music.

Icons Used in This Book

 I use this icon to offer suggestions based on my own experience. Or to tell you stories about some of the truly amazing cocktail parties I've attended. Or to tell you about some of the wild music I've run across at cocktail parties. Or. . . .

 You can't throw a cocktail party for free. But that doesn't mean that you can't cut a corner here or there without your guests knowing. This icon gives you some suggestions as to how.

If you believe in cosmic oneness, then you probably also believe that you're going to remember each and every word in this book. I hope so — but if not, this icon points out things you should definitely remember.

Let's be candid: Alcohol and some activities just don't mix. This icon serves to point out situations that are best avoided so your guests can be your guests again and again.

In addition to the alcohol-related concerns, this icon points out potentially foolhardy or unwise ideas that may otherwise escape your attention.

This icon points out extra little touches to make your parties most memorable. Cheers!

Where to Go from Here

Don't know where to start? Pick a topic, find the chapter on that subject, and dive in. Or just turn the page. Again, with this book, where you start really doesn't matter. What does matter is that you have a memorable party and join the growing cocktail movement. Enjoy!

Part I

Basic

Considerations

"You and your 'Running-With-The-Bulls-at-Pamplona Party.' Let's just hope the bull gets tired before the guacamole dries up."

In this part...

A friend of mine used to be a newspaper
reporter. No matter how well the friend's
stories were written, they all pretty much began
with the answers to the same six questions:
Who? What? When? Where? Why? How?

Most of those same questions are important to
ask when planning a cocktail party. Why do you
want to throw a party? What kind of party are
you going to have? Who are you going to invite?
When is the party going to be? And where will
you have the party?

These answers lay the foundation for a great
party. What about the "how" part? That's what
the rest of the book is for!

Chapter 1

What Kind of Party Are You Going to Have?

- -

In This Chapter

▶ Big or small?

▶ What's the budget?

▶ Who to invite?

▶ When to have it?

- -

*C*hoosing the type of cocktail party to have is the first decision that you have to make. You must decide who's coming to your party and then decide what type of party will work best. And give yourself plenty of time: Six months ahead is not too soon to be mulling over ideas.

How Big a Party Do You Want?

I've thrown cocktail parties for six people, and I've thrown cocktail parties for six thousand people. Both kinds can be wonderful experiences that people talk about for months. But keep in mind that you must weigh certain factors when making that "Big or small?" decision.

The small party

A small gathering of people — six to ten — can be nice, intimate, relaxed, and friendly. Everyone gets a chance to talk and gets to know each other. You can pay attention to everyone. A small party is less stressful and much less expensive. You can throw the party at your home and stash the coats on the master bed.

At a small party, it's crucial that the invited guests all show up, as you don't want to end up with only three people. All the guests must like each other, have things in common, and be able to carry on a conversation because they'll have fewer people to intermingle with. You still want to think about the *flow* of your party, or the traffic pattern your guests will likely take (discussed more in Chapter 6). You can give the guests a chance to have a few drinks and surprise them by introducing a couple different hors d'oeuvres or desserts.

If you're new to entertaining, start small. By the time you've given three or four small parties, you'll be confident enough to jump right into a bigger party.

The overflow flowed

I recently sang at an exclusive cocktail party at a new restaurant, lounge, and cigar bar. The basement was filled with pool tables, the main floor was for dining. Upstairs there was a large lounge and cigar bar, which featured a woman rolling Cuban cigars (a legal practice in Canada) in the corner. What amazed me was that after a very brief pause at the front door, you could move freely throughout the huge venue. Every room was comfortably full, and while the stairways and halls were slightly crowded, people kept moving.

The secret to the flow of the party? The entertainment happened at different times in different places, virtually unannounced. The furniture was arranged so that even with a thick crowd, people could move from one corner of the room to another easily. The drinks were free, but each floor specialized in a different one (martini lounge, champagne bar, scotch tasting area, and wine floor) and had hors d'oeuvres that went well with the drink.

The big party

You have fewer concerns about individual chemistries between guests at a big party and more concerns about overall ambiance and atmosphere. At a large party, you must create atmosphere and multiple spaces for your guests so they can mingle, play, and generally have a fabulous time.

The big party is more work, of course, and as a host, you will find having lengthy conversations with any one guest difficult. Your job is to stage manage the flow of the party and to try and see that the party takes on a life of its own.

What Is Your Budget?

Every party I've ever thrown has had one constant: a bill. No matter what the size of your party, you're going to have a few bills to pay. And not all of those costs are obvious.

When you're planning your party, keep these items in mind:

- ✔ **Venue.** If you're throwing a party at home, the venue (party location) won't be an additional cost. If you want to throw a party somewhere else, however, the owner is going to expect to be paid. See Chapter 2.

- ✔ **Invitations.** As you can read in Chapter 5, invitations make the first impression on your guests. You don't have to spend a great deal of time on invitations, but you do have to budget time — and money — for them. And don't forget postage!

- ✔ **Decorations.** Ambiance is a critical factor at a cocktail party. A few checkered flags make all the difference when you have an automobile racing theme, for example. See Chapter 6 for hints and suggestions.

- ✔ **Entertainment.** You may have the sound that you want for your party already in your CD collection — or not. Or do you want a DJ, or a band? I have some tips on what to look for in Chapter 7.

- ✔ **Food and liquor.** Okay, food and liquor are obvious costs, but exactly how much should you budget? I have some recommendations on that in Chapters 8 and 9.

- ✔ **Equipment.** Do you have enough chairs? Enough tables? What about glassware? You'll find tips on making or renting throughout the book.

One other budget category deserves mention: staffing. If you're only doing a small party of up to twenty people, then you can certainly do everything yourself or with a friend. One of you can greet guests, take coats, and pass out hors d'oeuvres. The other can be the bartender and change the music when necessary.

If you're putting on a larger party, you may be able to get friends to volunteer to help. If not, consider hiring a coat checker, a bartender, door security, a sound and lighting person, a disc jockey, a caterer, or dancers.

Remember, if this party is your first, don't jump in too deep; you're better off to start small. Keep track of your costs, and you'll have a better idea of expenses for future parties.

Who Do You Wish to Invite?

You can spend days hauling white sand into your backyard for an authentic beach party, but if the chemistry isn't right at the party, then the party just won't click into gear.

How do you make sure that the chemistry is right? By inviting people who match what you want the party to achieve, and by inviting people who mesh well, because a cocktail party is all about people conversing and mingling.

The right people for the right party

Be clear about the reasons you're giving this party. What are your intentions? Is the party for a small group of old friends? For a special occasion? For the employees at work? Are you trying to match up some single friends? Are you trying to say thank you to a staff that has labored long and hard on a movie or video? Is the party really just for fun, or do you have a hidden agenda, like a business deal or a new relationship? Or are you putting on a party for the sheer pleasure of giving others a great and memorable time?

After you determine the reason for the party, you need to clarify that each guest on the list falls into that "reason." You don't have to invite every single friend and neighbor; make sure that each guest adds something and that his or her presence is for a reason other than just knowing you. Table 1-1 gives you some guidelines.

Table 1-1		The Party Decision Maker	
Reason for	*Party Size*	*People Who Should Be Invited*	*People Who Party Shouldn't Be Invited*
To thank staff	30	The staff!	Business clients

Reason for Party	Party Size	People Who Should Be Invited	People Who Shouldn't Be Invited
Kevin's birthday	20	Close friends	Kevin's ex-girlfriend and her new boyfriend
Melleny and Clive's anniversary	60+	Ten Elvis imperson-ators, family, a few of Clive's clients, closest friends	Complete strangers
To finalize a deal	Small	The client	Nonessential staff members

You don't always have to invite the obvious choices. For example, if the reason for the party is to honor a certain person, and you're hosting, then keeping the guest of honor's guest list in mind is important. However, while you want to make the guest of honor happy, a successful party is much more important. Therefore, if you can't include everyone on the guest of honor's guest list, then so be it. Also, it's not improper to have a few guests who haven't met the guest of honor, as long as that number is limited.

Where there's a will, there's a hobo

JAVMZ SAYZ The host must know when a party crasher is welcome and when he must be turned away. I don't normally go to places where I'm not invited, but I crashed lots of big parties in my younger years.

No story has a happier ending than the time I crashed a record superstore's grand opening party. I had crashed a private staff party a few weeks earlier, where I won the "Entertainer of the Night" honors at their karaoke contest doing "I Am Woman" by Helen Reddy. I took home a cheesy trophy, engraved and dated by the store.

The day of the superstore opening party, I got designer Melleny Melody to create a hobo suit for me. She glued old subway transfers on the shoulders and cigarette butts

(continued)

(continued)

on the lapels. I carried a garbage bag over my shoulder and wore a sign around my neck that said "Not Invited." When I arrived at the party, the news cameras and curious pedestrians gathered around me to look at my trophy. "I was somebody a few weeks ago — now, I guess I'm a nobody!" I whined jokingly. In less than twenty minutes, the president of the company came out and personally brought me in. Once inside, I excused myself to use the washroom. I had a pressed tux in the garbage bag over my shoulder, so I changed attire and then mingled.

The happy ending? Paul Alofs, the president of the company, later moved to BMG and signed me to a big record contract!

The right people for each other

When you're making a cocktail, you can't just throw different kinds of liquor into a glass and assume that the results will be spectacular. Likewise, you can't just assume that you're going to throw a group of people together and they're automatically going to have a good time. Choose people who you think will enjoy each other's company.

One of the critical considerations in party chemistry is the size of the guest list. If you're only talking about 12 to 20 people, then you need to be concerned with the various minor chemical makeups: Who's mad at whom? Who broke up with whom last year? Who's having an affair with whom?

If the party is larger, 30-plus people, and people have room to move around and get away, then the individual personal dramas are less of a concern. They may actually add to the excitement and gossip quotient of your party.

Also consider a few of the following questions:

- ✔ **Singles or couples?** You want some couples, of course, but singles most often make a cocktail party interesting. Try to get a good balance of both.

- ✔ **Yin or yang?** Always keep the male to female ratio in mind. If you know that two of your single female friends are showing up, then you can use that as an enticement to get a couple of single male friends, or vice versa. Then use their attendance as an enticement to get other singles.

Try to keep the yin/yang ratio close, but it's better to have a few extra women than too many men. Men act more dignified and less Neanderthal when outnumbered by women.

✔ **Introverts or extroverts?** Remember, conversing and mingling is what cocktail parties are all about, so you need enough extroverts to put some life into the party, but good talkers need good listeners.

A word about extroverts: When you're putting on a party, you want some spice. Maybe you know a few people who are loud and flamboyant and like to wear lamp shades on their heads. You may not want to see them every day, but you very well may want them at your party.

To get the party moving quickly, invite a few of your extroverted guests to come over a little early. You can always offer them a hot meal or a special drink as an incentive to get there before the others.

✔ **Friend or foe?** Think about commonalities between people and potential new friends. If a potential guest isn't your favorite person, think about putting differences aside for the sake of your party.

Sir Spinner Fine Vinyl and I once co-hosted a party for Timothy Leary. One fellow I knew had apparently said some unkind things about me, but he was knee-deep in virtual reality and had read everything that Leary had ever written. My intuition told me to swallow my pride and invite this ornery gent. It was a great move. He asked Leary the most intelligent questions of the evening, and we've since become friends.

If the party consists of a group of friends, try and bring in some new people who don't know each other. Doing so adds to the interest and gives people a chance to add to their circle of friends.

✔ **Young or old?** For certain parties, try to keep your guests within a 10-year age span. For parties of enthusiasts with specialized interests, the interest or hobby creates the commonality, and age won't matter as much.

> ✔ **Shop talk or non-shop talk?** If you invite one of your co-workers, do you have to invite them all? And if you do that, is everyone going to be talking about work? BORING. If a fair amount of your co-workers are invited guests, don't forget to get some conversationalists there to liven things up with other topics as well. Again, this is where you need a small legion of extroverts to work the room — party consultants, dance instigators, and out-going talkers. As host, your main duty is near the front door until most of the guests have arrived, but at times you may have to dart around the room to make sure that people are mingling and enjoying themselves.
>
> The host must try to keep things informal and get people onto topics that are not work-related. If you are not comfortable with this duty, hire someone to act as co-host and have her introduce new people and new topics into a conversation.

If you know of someone who will really make your party special, then try to entice her in any way you can. My first offer is always free drinks, but drinks are often free at small cocktail parties anyway. Occasionally, I will pay up to $50 or $100 if the guest is a great dancer who promises to work the room and make sure that wallflowers don't grow by the dancing area. Perhaps you know an entertainer like a comedian or mentalist.

If you're putting on a party for a select group of people, such as employees from a company, consider hiring some actors to pull some type of prank or act as storytellers with tales from the rain forests of Africa. Something unusual and unexpected gives the guests something to talk about.

I once threw a party where I had the waitress and bartender join me in a song. We had rehearsed it, but we made it look as if it was totally impromptu. Another time, I hired a few comedians to impersonate me. They had a bunch of my key phrases and mannerisms perfected, and they mingled through the room, telling people they had a book and record coming out, they were working on a film script, and so on. After twenty minutes, someone finally noticed that four people in the room claimed to be doing exactly what I was doing. We awarded the observant guest a glass of champagne and a round of cheers!

Special talents make for special parties

Do you have a friend with talent who may liven up your party? Maybe she makes balloon animals or knows lots of card tricks. You don't want to put your guests on the spot, but maybe someone you know has unusual talents. Perhaps you have a friend who is double-jointed and does contortions while tying cherry stems in knots with his tongue. Something fun can be an ice-breaker at a party.

Inner politics with your guest list

If you can avoid getting bogged down in politics, invite the people you want at your party and don't invite people that you don't want at your party. It sounds redundant, but it's that simple. If you can't invite the whole office, inform your co-workers in advance that your space is limited and that you hope they understand. You don't want uninvited co-workers to hear this news from someone else.

If you are meek enough to inherit the Earth and don't want to deal with this dilemma, you can always use a pseudonym for the invitation. For example, "Art Vandelay Invites You to Attend a Cocktail Party for (YOUR NAME)." Then if your friends ask why they weren't invited, you can answer that Art must've made the mistake! Dishonest, but some people would rather lie than offend.

Just when you think you are through the politics of your own list, your DJ, bartender, and doorman all have a few friends they'd like to bring. Wrong! When you first discuss the party with your staff (or helpful friends), make it clear what kind of event it is. If your bartender is a volunteer, he may insist on bringing a date to assist — that's obviously a different story. Regardless, deal with the political issues early on so you can forget about them long before party time!

If you have more than one host, discuss your duties and make sure that someone is on the political issue.

Most Important: When to Have the Party

Setting the date is one of the most important things you can do in order to make your party really happen. Just the mere act of circling the date on your calendar — and verbalizing to a few friends that you are really having the party — serves to put your own wheels in motion. If you've already put on a few parties, a couple of weeks notice may be enough time. But if you're putting on your first, give yourself at least a month to plan. If you have a specific venue in mind, you may need even more time than that. See Chapter 10 for more details and suggestions.

Setting the date

Look at a calendar. Do you have a date in mind already? If so, ask yourself these questions:

✔ Does the date coincide with a holiday? Parties around holidays can be good or bad, depending on whether people are likely to have other plans and/or whether the holiday puts people in the party spirit.

A three-day weekend or a major holiday can mean that people are committed to their families or are going out of town. On the other hand, New Year's Eve is a traditional party time.

If you are having a party on a holiday, get your invitations out as early as possible so guests can schedule appropriately.

✔ Does the date conflict with a major concert or festival in your town? Consult your local entertainment listings and check on that date.

✔ Does the party conflict with family holidays or once-in-a-lifetime-type events? Of course, this really has a great deal to do with the reputation of your parties. After you throw a few of them, your party may be considered an event worth deserting family for.

Once you've narrowed dates down to the week, you need to think about the day. If you already have your venue or location locked in, the day is a little less crucial. If you're renting a venue (discussed more in Chapter 2), then you're going to have more trouble getting a Friday or Saturday. If you really don't want to entertain people all night, weekdays do offer a certain advantage.

On a weekday — being a work or school night for many — most people are very happy to show up for a couple hours before heading home. Your challenge is to break up the monotony of their work day by offering engaging conversation, refreshing beverages, and the promise of new friends and some tasty snacks.

Which weekday? Let people get past the middle of the work week. By Thursday or Friday, they'll be heading into the weekend and will be in a much better mood.

If you're really going all out on your party, make sure that you book it on a night when you have the most factors on your side. If you're talking about a once-a-year bash where many people will be assisting you in getting things together, then by all means have the party on a weekend when people will be free to give you their undivided help.

If you end up choosing a weekday, plan on taking the day off. I can guarantee that something will come up every time, and you'll need the whole day to get ready.

Full moon factor

Entertainers who play every night claim that they can feel the difference in the air around the full moon. The crowds are a little crazier and more intense. Police and hospitals claim the same thing. So, depending on what you're trying to achieve with your party, keep the lunar factor in mind, too.

What time should the party be?

Remember, a cocktail party is *not* a dinner party, so you want to time it accordingly. Having cocktail parties in the early evening — 6 to 8 or 7 to 9 — is fairly standard. If the party is in the early evening on a weekday downtown, then you want to catch people on their way home from work. If the party is out at a suburban location, then you should make the time later. But if you do make it later, then have it start at 8 or later, so your guests don't arrive expecting dinner.

For certain occasions, you can also have a morning or midday cocktail party. These both, however, call for low-alcohol drinks along with mocktails and smartinis. Recipes and information on mocktails can be found in Chapter 8.

If you're having the party on a weekend, you need to decide if you are creating a stop on the way to a movie or another date, or if the party is the prime destination of the evening itself. A cocktail party on Friday from 5 to 7 works very well; people are ready to get a start on the weekend. A Saturday night party works best as the *destination location* — a party that goes into the night.

Whatever time you decide upon, have both the beginning and ending times on your invitation. At a cocktail party, the times listed on the invitation are considered to be the time the party begins and ends.

Recruit some help, and reward your recruits

Who will plan the party with you? Your friend, your brother, your sister, a co-worker, or your next-door neighbor? Anyone you get along with is a candidate. Working and sharing the adventure with someone else is more fun.

Sharing is especially important if you're organizing a larger event and recruiting friends to help. Give them a little of the excitement of the early planning stages. Have them help you set the date and time and help you keep track of all of those other little details. This not only guarantees they'll be available when you need them, but by keeping them informed of the details, they can talk the party up! And be sure to share the kudos when the party is all over.

Chapter 2

Where Do You Want to Have Your Party?

. . . .

In This Chapter

▶ Should you party at home or somewhere else

▶ What to keep in mind when you party at home

▶ What to keep in mind when you party somewhere else

▶ Legal considerations

. . . .

*O*ne of the most important decisions that you make regarding your cocktail party is picking the right *venue* — where to have the party. The perfect location can almost save or cover up for a poorly planned party. With this book as your handy guide, you're going to have plenty of time for every detail, so make location a big priority.

That location can certainly be your home, provided you give the matter some forethought. *Time* is the key word here. If you take the time to think about the issues of having the party at your place or finding the right venue, and take care of everything in advance, then you'll be able to relax a bit at your party, too. If you're having fun, then your guests will have a better time.

Home versus Venue

Deciding whether to have your party at home or somewhere else almost naturally follows the big questions in Chapter 1 — how big a party do you want, what's your budget, and where will the party be? You'll probably want to consider a cocktail party at home if

✔ **Your entire party budget won't buy you groceries for the month.** If this is the case, you probably don't want to spend money renting a venue.

✔ **You can count all of the guests on either your fingers or toes.** Why bother renting a venue for half a dozen people?

✔ **The main reason for having the party is to close a business deal.** If you still have some negotiating to do, you may not need the distractions of a larger venue.

✔ **You're meeting your prospective in-laws for the first time.** They'll want to focus on you, not the locale. Just make certain that you clean the house thoroughly first!

Likewise, lots of parties beg you to find just the right spot:

✔ **The theme's the thing, and you haven't got the theme thing.** If you're going to throw a '70s retro party, you need a dance floor. If you don't have a dance floor, you have to find a place that does — unless you want to hang that shiny disco ball in your garage. I didn't think so.

✔ **You've invited the Mormon Tabernacle Choir.** They don't need a tabernacle for nothing. And they're probably really nice people. Just remember to have lots of non-alcoholic drinks available.

✔ **You don't want to clean up the mess.** Cleanup costs often are included in venue rental fees. And with some parties, paying someone else to mop and vacuum is a bargain.

✔ **You adore your privacy and don't know some of your guests.** Allowing someone into your home is very revealing. Many people would rather entertain elsewhere and keep their private lives from the public.

Don't make the mistake of starting off at too grand a scale. Nothing is worse than having a load of overhead expenses and waiting for more people to arrive while watching your sister, her boyfriend, and your old high school chum hovering over the deli table. If you've never put on a cocktail party, then start small. After you get it down and have a few successful ones, then your friends will fight to come to your parties.

Throwing the Party at Home

If you have not seen *The Party,* a '60s film starring Peter Sellers, go out this minute and rent it on video. After you've seen it, imagine your home being destroyed by a "bad-luck-Schleprock party crasher." If you party proof your pad (more on that in Chapter 6), and have invitations RSVP'd (see Chapter 5), you shouldn't have any problems.

Try to keep things simple if you throw a party at home. I've seen performance artists nearly burn the house down, cooks who create nauseating odors, and home power fuses blown by bands. Also, while guests rarely deliberately damage property, you and your bartender should monitor your guests' drinking, to prevent a drunk person from breaking things or hurting himself.

Is your house the proper place?

Having a party at home is just a little more complicated than inviting people over. In addition to whether or not you have enough space (discussed in the very next section), consider:

- ✔ **Are your walls fairly soundproofed?** Not only do you run the risk of disturbing your neighbors; if they're combative, you run the risk they'll play "battle of the bands" with their stereo and disrupt your party.

- ✔ **Do you have enough electrical power?** If you're planning live entertainment (see Chapter 7), you either need several power outlets that are on different circuits in convenient locations or your own portable generator.

- ✔ **Do you have a place for a bar that's near running water, and that is easily accessible?**

- ✔ **Is your place in a convenient location?** If you live in the suburbs and every one of your guests lives downtown, how will they get to your party? Are you near public transit and is parking available in the area?

Do you have enough space?

Take a good look at your available space. If you remove or rearrange furniture, how many people can you accommodate — standing around chatting with drink in hand? You need to do a little math in your head. You want this "standing room only" to be full but still open enough that people can move freely about and wander off to get another drink. Here are some rough guidelines:

- ✔ All standing — 6 square feet per person
- ✔ Some seated — 8 square feet per person

✔ Dance area (if needed) — 6 square feet plus per person

✔ Bar area (if not the kitchen counter) — 100 square feet

✔ Upright piano — 50 square feet

✔ Grand piano — 100 square feet

✔ Band — 100 square feet (jazz trio or small combo); 400 square feet (big band orchestra)

What about the neighbors?

Your house is not the only one affected when you host a party, and good cocktail etiquette calls for checking with your neighbors first. Maybe the senior citizens next door will call the police, or maybe you'll be disturbing sleeping babies in the room below. Don't leave this situation to turn into a crisis on the night of the party. Talk to your neighbors well in advance, and try to accommodate them. If your neighbors do have a problem during the party, at least they will know — because you talked to them in advance — that they can come over and talk to a reasonable person.

Most people will tolerate some noise and inconvenience as long as they're warned in advance, and perhaps invited. Of course, you never want to feel obligated to invite anyone to your party — the person must add some spice to it.

What about safety?

If you have a swimming pool, you must have a non-drinking friend act as lifeguard. Alcohol and swimming make a lousy combo. Make sure that your guests pose no danger to themselves or others before allowing them into the pool.

The same can be said for slippery floors, things people may trip over, and so on. If you are holding the party at your home or at a friend's, check your insurance policy to make sure that you are covered. If not, you may want to seriously consider booking it elsewhere.

Don't cross the (tan) line

JAYMZ SAYZ The police showed up at a party I once threw in Basel, Switzerland, where topless sun-bathing was common. The officers seemed to be on the verge of laughing while I nervously asked them what the problem was. It seems they answered a call from a neighbor in a large apartment building across the field who claimed that people were sunbathing in the nude and that some kind of orgy was in progress.

To show the police, she took a chair and placed it against the wall. She couldn't actually see the party out of the window unless she stood on the chair, because it was a small sun window. But with the officers watching, she climbed on her tippy toes and shouted, "There they are — I can see them — it's disgusting!"

The officer telling the story said he got on the chair and saw people dancing and two topless girls sunbathing on their stomachs. The police were kind to warn me of my nosy neighbor — but had this been a toga theme party, the cops may have shown more concern.

Throwing the Party at a Venue

The most exciting cocktail parties take place in a setting that seems a bit foreign or exotic — someplace a little bit different. The right location makes your friends feel playful, uninhibited, and childlike. That doesn't mean that you have to fly everyone off to a tropical paradise island, but it does mean you have to spend some time in search of the right locale. Take a day or two and check out locations. With a little phone work and legwork, you can find the right exotic locale in your own city or town.

JAYMZ SAYZ In general, utilizing an already established place is easier than throwing your party where no one has gone before, so to speak. If you find a potential venue you like, get the owner or manager's name. But don't stop there — continue searching until you feel you know what else is out there. Leave yourself with more than one option. Your dream locale may be shut down by the liquor board or go bankrupt two days before your party.

Venue economics 101

Let me be very clear: Unless you borrow a friend's apartment or throw the party at home, you must have money. Venue owners make money from the rent (if any) that they charge you for your party, and from three other sources:

- ✔ **Booze.** Alcohol sales are the primary source of income for a bar owner. Bartenders like nothing more than a lively crowd that drinks a great deal. If you can pack a room with people and let the bar owner have the liquor income, she'll be happy and you'll be happy.

- ✔ **Food.** A bar owner isn't really going to look at the food as a major source of revenue, but if you're planning on serving food — even an hors d'oeuvre tray — then check and see if the kitchen can prepare it for you and add a little to their revenue. If they can't, they will probably allow you to bring a caterer in, but always check with them first.

- ✔ **The door income.** In general, the door income (after any admissions taxes) is used to pay for entertainment. In rooms that have live music, the bands usually pay a usage fee for the sound system and lights and then receive the bulk of the door income. So, if you bring in a large number of people who buy drinks, the bulk of the door receipts (at least 80 percent) should be yours.

  Although most clubs follow this unwritten rule, a real hot spot may not. Your percentage of the door is open to negotiation in most popular clubs. A venue with the capacity for 300 will likely be happy to throw a private party for 150–200, whereas a smaller venue with the capacity for 80 will likely want the room legally full.

  Just because the bulk of the door income is yours doesn't mean that you'll be allowed to run the door. A bar owner is usually very concerned about underage people entering and will want his own staff on the door. You will, however, be allowed to stand up front and work with the door staff.

How these types of income affect your party plans depends on the type of room you want to rent.

The economics of entertaining big kids

I threw a retirement party for Mr. Dressup, the most famous children's entertainer in Canada. After almost 30 years of watching him on television (I'm a big kid), I thought the least I could do is throw him a party at one of Toronto's most elegant hotels.

I had originally planned a dinner party, but decided at the last minute that most of his biggest fans couldn't afford the meal, so I turned it into a free cocktail party with a cash bar. Suddenly, the agreement I had with the hotel for the past month meant nothing, and we had to re-negotiate less than a week before the event! I gave them a two thousand dollar deposit, and owed them the same amount at the end of the evening if their bar sales did not reach a certain plateau.

In the end, my guests spent a lot of money on drinks — and several national TV networks were present — so the manager didn't ask for the second payment. But had my guests been teetotalers, I would have had to pay through the nose. Make sure that you don't end up in that situation!

The usual suspects

Three types of rooms are most commonly rented for cocktail parties — reception halls and the like; bars without live entertainment; and bars with live entertainment. Remember, renting an established place is easier. But that doesn't mean it always goes smoothly.

Sometimes the best venues can be the worst to deal with! In the spring of '97 I had a record launch cocktail party for one of my albums, *ClintEastWoodyAllenAlda.* I picked a Toronto location where all the famous celebrities go, thinking that was the classiest joint in town. Well, the party and concert were fun, but I had to deal with lots of unpleasant surprises with the venue. I had to use a union sound team, the members of which seemed to hate their job (and my music); the waiters were lazy and unpleasant; and the manager of the room billed me for things that were not in the contract — for example, four hundred dollars to turn the power on in the room. Luckily, my party consulting partner for this event was Gino Empry, Tony Bennett's former manager. He managed to keep the surprise costs down, but nevertheless it was a hair-pulling experience.

Don't let these kinds of misunderstandings happen to you. Let me help you understand the nature of the place you're looking at.

Ballrooms, VFW, reception halls, and the like

Guiding principle: Strictly in the business of renting out space for wedding receptions, dances, and other events.

Economic implication: The rental fee can be steep, because these venues don't have the bar as a source of income.

Things to keep in mind during negotiations: Rental fees can go down drastically if you give the venue a chance to make some money elsewhere. If you find one of these rooms, ask if they have a liquor license, in-house catering, and such. Perhaps it's a hotel where you can put up some of your entertainers or special guests.

A bar that does not feature live entertainment

Guiding principle: The "neighborhood bar." It's the hangout.

Economic implication: This kind of bar must have what is called *room draw.* That means people go there and hang out and spend money. The owner has worked very hard to establish a room draw and a clientele that calls his place home. That clientele is his bread and butter, while you are going to do your party one night and then be gone. If he loses his steady customers, he's in real trouble.

Things to keep in mind during negotiations: You may be able to utilize the room, but not during the prime time. You'll have to ask, "Is there a day or time that isn't very busy for you that I could have a private party in here? I expect to pack the place." You will be thought much more professional if you talk numbers. How many people are expected? Are they heavy drinkers? Don't exaggerate, as owners and managers will expect you to deliver your estimated numbers.

A bar that does feature live entertainment

Guiding principle: To be a *destination location,* which means that people are going there because of what's going on.

Economic implication: In most cases, a venue with live entertainment is trying to figure out how to get people into the room in order to sell them drinks. Management is trying to draw from different crowds — different *scenes* — of people on different nights. That's why you'll sometimes see places with schedules like the following:

- ✔ Sunday — Jazz
- ✔ Monday — Karaoke
- ✔ Tuesday — '70s Disco dance
- ✔ Wednesday — '80s New Wave dance
- ✔ Thursday — Ladies Night: Buff Oiled Men
- ✔ Friday and Saturday — Hot local rock band whose audience drinks a lot
- ✔ Sunday — Sumo wrestling or electric buckin' bulls

If the room is packed and the door admission pays for the live entertainment, then the owner will be pleased with the bar income. If the room is dead and the owner has to dip into his bar income to pay the band, he won't be happy.

What to keep in mind during negotiations: If you can guarantee a larger crowd than one of their regular nights, then you likely can have the room if they can sell the drinks.

Where else will I find what I'm looking for?

So the usual suspects don't interest you. Where else can you look? Everywhere. You may already know about a restaurant out by the airport where the waitresses still have beehive hairdos, a boat dock where you can have an outside barbecue, a karaoke bar in Chinatown, or a cottage where you can burn Tiki torches. If not, you can let your fingers do the walking in the phone book under *Halls and Auditoriums,* or simply take a drive around town. Here are a few places to consider:

✔ **An old hotel.** Classic old hotels can sometimes work very well for a cocktail party. Look through the phone book under *Hotels* or *Motels*. Make a list of the addresses of the older ones. Maybe they have a small ballroom or a great-looking lobby; perhaps the hotel bar itself has the desired look. Just remember, if you make the owner money, he is going to be happy to accommodate you. It's as simple as that.

✔ **A roadside motel.** Motels with the right look can often be found on old highways, and may have a great pool and patio with checkered tile or a great-looking wet bar. You can rent a block of rooms so guests can stay overnight. Remember, if you buy a block of rooms and give the owner/manager guaranteed revenue, chances are she will let you utilize more of the motel's services without paying extra.

✔ **An art gallery.** The concerns at a gallery are quite simple: The owner will appreciate the extra revenue, but will be very concerned about smoke and spilled drinks and damage done to his beautiful space and art. With some care and planning, you can alleviate the concerns. In all likelihood, the gallery will not have a liquor license, and you will have to make the proper arrangements.

✔ **The lobby of a theater.** You may find a beautifully restored vaudeville theater with a gorgeous lobby. This venue can work, but it may be expensive. Your party has to take place at a time that doesn't disrupt the current scheduling of shows taking place at the theater.

✔ **A bowling alley.** Bowling alleys can provide a built-in ambiance that may be great for your party. A bowling alley usually has a license to at least sell beer, may have a bar with hard liquor, and may also have special banquet rooms that can be rented.

✔ **A skating rink.** Rinks are usually geared more toward a younger crowd, and they may not have a liquor license. But if you like the space and the potential a rink offers, then check with the manager about what's been done before and what is possible.

✔ **A pool hall.** The entertainment at a pool hall can mesh well with a cocktail party — fun, yet something people in nice attire can participate in. Most pool halls also have a few arcade games, and perhaps a shuffle- or dartboard. The down side is that you may have to pay a security deposit, as billiard tables are easy to destroy. You'll require extra security if the party is big — including someone to make sure that the regulars don't crash the party. Also, someone should keep his eyes on the tables, reminding guests not to place drinks or cigarettes anywhere near the tables. And many of your guests will play rather than mingle.

Looking over the venue

You've found the right venue, one that is just perfect for your party. But consider these things before you book:

✔ **How many people can be accommodated?** Do your guests have enough room — or too much?

Always have your party in a place that can fill up. Packing a room that is slightly too small is much better than looking dead in a big room. A cocktail party is supposed to be an intimate group of friends laughing and chatting. Better too crowded than not.

✔ **Are tables and chairs available, if needed?**

✔ **Are the kitchen and refrigeration areas available for prepping and storage?** And, if needed, can you use the venue's kitchenware?

✔ **Are the bathrooms clean and large enough?** Never underestimate the impression that a bathroom can make on your guests. (I talk more about this in Chapter 6.)

✔ **Is the coat storage adequate?**

✔ **Can people smoke, or are separate rooms available for smoking and nonsmoking guests?**

✔ **What decorating is permitted?** And when can you get into the room to start decorating?

If you have found a perfect location that doesn't look quite right, don't distress. You can usually change the look of a place for your event if you are professional and willing to pay a bit more to put things back in order. You may need to remove neon beer signs and advertising. Talk to the owner or manager in advance about your needs and how and where you can store things carefully. Show the owner some respect and courtesy, and she will show you the same.

✔ **Does the venue have a sound system and/or microphones and/or a stage?** Clubs often rent, rather than own, their sound systems, because the technology changes all the time and — with bands coming in and out — the owner or manager really wants someone else to be in charge of it. Rental is usually cheaper on weekdays than weekends, but expect to pay something if the sound system is nice. See Chapter 7 for more on music.

✔ **Does the club have a disk jockey?** Disc jockeys are also usually freelance employees. They probably carry their own records and rotate between different clubs. Usually the DJ plays from his own record collection in a given club. If you hear a DJ that you like, catch him at a break and get his card or phone number. See if he's available to spin at your cocktail party. Ask if he owns his own turntable and mixer or just records? See what he provides and what you need to provide to utilize his services. (DJs are covered more thoroughly in Chapter 7.)

✔ **Are the lighting arrangements acceptable?** Some clubs have good lighting; some don't. One club will have four little pink spots that are either on or off; another club will have fog machines, strobe lights, a mirror ball, and all kinds of fancy chase lights. Often the house sound man deals with the lighting, too, but in a room that has state-of-the-art production, you may have a separate lighting person. See Chapter 6 for more on lighting.

✔ **Have you done parties at that venue before?** Did it work? Was the party a success and did you receive any compliments about the choice of venues? Did the owner or manager thank you at the end of the night?

✔ **Does the venue have a reputation for private events?** You can always ask the manager for references, but keep in mind that he'll likely give you the number of his aunt or a regular customer who threw a shindig there once.

✔ **Does the building owner have insurance?** Who's responsible for what? Make sure that this is specified in the contract.

✔ **What's the neighborhood like?** Sometimes the best old, classic venues are now in areas of town that are less than desirable. You are going to have to assess for yourself if the area is just a bit run down or outright dangerous. If you've found the perfect location in a bad area of town, maybe you can work out shuttle transportation to your party; maybe you can have your larger male friends escort the ladies to their cars afterward. Consider hiring more security.

If you sense that anything illegal is taking place right in the venue itself, chances are good that the activity is being condoned by the owner or management. Keep this fact in mind when making your location decision.

You know you're at the wrong place when . . .

The top five signs that you are looking at the wrong place:

1. A chalk outline is still visible on the dance floor.

2. A little kid outside tells you he's having a two-for-one sale on handguns.

3. The burned-out car in front of the place was a police car.

4. The owner has a tattoo that says "Mother," and his mother has one that says "Born to raise heck."

5. The manager has not one, not two, but three pit bulls.

Closing the deal

Okay, now that you know a little bit about how a bar or club operates, you're ready to think about booking the place.

Approaching the owner or manager

You're ready to talk to the manager. Remember that people who work in bars often come to resent the ringing phone and sometimes even ignore it. You may leave ten messages and never hear back from them. You will do better by showing up in the mid- to late afternoon, 2 or 3 p.m., and hanging out until you can get a word in.

Most importantly, remember that you are offering the room a full house of happy people buying alcohol. If the room already does well on weekends, you may have trouble getting a Friday or Saturday, but check anyway. If the answer is still no, but you absolutely have to have that room on a weekend, you can try a party before the room's doors open, say from 4 to 6 p.m. In my experience, however, few people ever attend an indoor cocktail party during these hours.

Many room rentals will be on a handshake

Many venue managers will not sign a contract, because they are used to working in an environment where things can drastically change overnight. The good news is that if you have to blow off your engagement, you won't lose a big deposit. The bad news is that the same thing can happen to you. You increase your odds of things going smoothly if you act confident and professional.

When you approach the owner or manager, say that you want to confirm a room-use agreement. Have a piece of paper on which you have written what you understand the room is providing and what you understand that you will provide. Quickly go over the details one more time, and then tell the manager that you'd like to confirm. Your part of the conversation should go something like this:

> *"I'd like to confirm your room for my private party. I'll be providing a room full of happy people buying booze, and you'll be providing lights and a sound system. I'm going to pay your Wednesday DJ to spin for my party, and I'll pay your tech to help me hang up some decorations and to troubleshoot. I'll need to start setting up early afternoon right after your lunch hour. Can we confirm my party for Wednesday, May 23, from 9 to 1?"*

Make sure that the club owner or manager gets out her club calendar and writes down the date and time before you leave.

Once you've confirmed, always double-check right down to the last week. Stop by, have a drink, and say hello. In the world of clubs and alcohol, all kinds of unpredictable things can happen. A club may get a liquor violation and be shut down. A tax problem may put the club out of business on short notice. Maybe your party gets bumped because a big rock band wants to have their record release party the same night. Maybe you get bumped because a movie crew wants to film in the venue.

With everything, confirm and reconfirm. Remember, in the entertainment business, "confirmed" often means "confirmed unless a better opportunity to make money comes along."

I want to give some drinks away

If you rent a ballroom or hall, you may have no choice but to give drinks away, depending on liquor laws in your area.

But think about a *no-host* bar situation: You have certain people whom you want to receive free drinks, or maybe you want everyone that attends to receive her first two drinks free.

Free drinks will be something that you will want to clarify with the room manager, but the concept goes something like this: You issue some sort of tickets for free drinks. Be imaginative with the tickets. Perhaps instead of little pieces of paper, you'll want to hand out little plastic teeth or arcade tokens. Whatever the case, these tickets are good for a drink at the bar. What's crucial here is that you work out in advance how much you are paying for the drinks. At the end of the night, the tickets are counted and you have to pay for the drinks.

Complimentary drink tickets or tokens are not always dispersed equally. Some celebrities or members of the press may only stay as long as the freebies are flowing, simply because they are not accustomed to paying for things at parties, so you want to gauge how long you desire their presence and give them an appropriate number of tickets. Other people may provide entertainment value just by their presence. In a sense, they are "working the party." Just remember to be discreet if you are not giving everyone the same amount of drink tickets.

Maybe you'll pay full bar price; maybe you'll get a discount. Maybe the manager will throw in ten or fifteen drinks for free. It really all depends on the amount of people in attendance and how much revenue your party generates. If a great deal of money will be made, a bar owner will be more generous about a few free drinks here and there.

If you're planning something shocking, don't surprise the staff

Perhaps you want to have a marching band in loincloths parade through the venue. Maybe you think that the venue management is going to be shocked by your 7-foot-tall drag queen jumping out of a cake. Tell them beforehand. Just wait a bit. Book the room first, talk about other details, and then get around to mentioning the "specialties" after you've chatted a few times.

People that work in the entertainment business are jaded. They may not all look like it, but they like excitement and people. As long as they know that you're professional and that they aren't going to get shut down by the liquor board due to some activity at your party, they will go along with most anything. You just need to present your ideas to them in the right light.

Show me the money — and a little respect

Be nice to the people who really do the work. You will probably deal with the owner or the manager when you book a venue, but from that point on the janitor and the bartender and the sound man are your greatest allies. On the day that you set up for your party, the working staff are the people who know where the extra chairs and ladder are stored. They are the ones who will change a light bulb or the sign on the marquee; they are the ones that will help to handle an obnoxious drunk that wanders in off the street.

Your fun party is their job; you are creating extra work for them so the boss can make more money. Be nice to the people that really do the work, and they will help you when you really need it. Tip them if they go above and beyond for you; don't assume that the boss is taking care of them. If they're working at the party itself, let them know that they're welcome to some food. If your party is a great success and you want to host another one, these people will remember you and put in a good word with the owner or manager.

The Long Arm of the Law

Check and see what kind of licenses and permits are required in connection with your party. Laws regarding the serving of alcohol are very specific, and they need to be taken seriously. In many countries, the liquor control board is capable of shutting you down for violations. In general, liquor laws are more strict in North America than in Europe. Be aware of the laws and follow them.

A liquor store, party rental outfit, or liquor control board can probably give you the information that you need to be legal. Many of the permits must be obtained ahead of time and will cost a fee. Don't leave this detail until the last minute. Know the following:

- ✔ What are your state's or province's laws regarding the serving of liquor?
- ✔ What are the hours that you can serve?
- ✔ If you're booked into a venue or a hotel, can you provide your own liquor or does the venue need to serve?
- ✔ Who provides what and who pays?
- ✔ What permit do you need to serve liquor outdoors?
- ✔ How do you order liquor and have it delivered?

When you fill out your application for a banquet permit to serve liquor, you'll find a space that says *Purpose of the Party,* or somesuch. "Birthday party" or "Gathering of old friends" sounds better than "A re-enactment of the pre-war decadence of Berlin."

Depending on your party, other laws may affect you. Are you planning a fire on a beach? This activity may not be legal. If you're planning on offering games of chance, you may not get hassled, but know the law. If you want to put a sound system in a park, be aware of noise regulations. Check on ordinances so you don't get caught surprised.

If you're charging admission and providing entertainment, there may be amusement or admissions taxes that apply. You need to inquire and find out what is relevant to what you are doing and what you need to concern yourself with.

Friends don't let friends drive drunk

Recent court rulings have made *servers of alcohol* liable for automobile accidents that happened after the person(s) left the place where they had partaken. Exercise extreme caution. *Do not* let inebriated guests and friends leave your party and drive. You'll want your door person to stay on top of this situation. Set up designated drivers before hand.

If a guest is obnoxiously insistent on driving drunk, then quickly get a few other friends involved to help get his keys away from him. Remember the technique perfected by New York's 21 Club and use a "drunk" to persuade a drunk to do the right thing.

Part II
The Theme's the Thing

The 5th Wave   By Rich Tennant

Past Life Regression therapy group~7:00

"...and remember — this Friday you're all invited to my 'come-as-you-were' party."

In this part...

Ask people what they think of when they hear "cocktail party" and they'll probably start talking about tuxedoes and formal gowns and ballroom dancing and Fred Astaire and . . . you get the picture. True, that's one kind of cocktail party, but only one.

The most important factor in what kind of cocktail party you're going to have is the theme. Pick a good theme, and the rest of the party planning problems suddenly disappear. This section gives you tips on small and large parties. And, yes, I've included a theme with tuxedoes and formal gowns and ballroom dancing. . . .

Chapter 3

Themes for Small Parties and Special Occasions

A theme gives your cocktail party focus and allows you to really fine-tune the desired effect. Guests know what to expect and can dress in the spirit of the occasion — provided you give them some advance warning. For instance, if horned Viking helmets are required, your guests may have to book them in advance or rent them from the local opera company. Themes have another advantage: You'll find your guests are more likely to jump out of their shells (or horned Viking helmets) and into the fun in a temporary "theme" world.

Once you have a theme idea, give your party a name, an exciting name. "Tiki Torch Ball" sounds better than "Ernie's Cocktail Party." "Tribal Night Life Farewell" sounds far more exotic than "Wendy From Accounts Receivable's Going-Away Party." If you have trouble coming up with an exciting name, have a musician or an artistic friend help you come up with colorful words to describe your theme, and work those into a name. Of course, you can go *too far*. I once threw a New Year's Eve party called "The Tiki Lagoonism of Baghdadian Impactedness." In hindsight, *maybe* "Baghdadian Ecstasy" would have sufficed. Just maybe.

To get you started, this chapter has some tips on choosing a theme and then some ideas for smaller and special occasion parties, the kinds of cocktail parties you are most likely to make your first. Themes for larger parties can be found in Chapter 4.

Choosing a Theme

In order to choose a theme, you need to think about what your guests will most enjoy and your motives for throwing the party. Are you trying to impress your boss, a potential client, or a new in-law? Then a toga party is out!

A "Traditional Cocktail Party" may have elements of any of the themes listed here or in Chapter 4 (Elegant Soiree, American Backyard Barbecue, Tiki, or South of the Border). If you follow the book but don't wish to have a theme party, it's no less a cocktail party; it's just that you may have missed a great opportunity to enhance and personalize your get-together.

Here are some things to consider when choosing your theme:

- ✔ **How many guests will you have?** Intimate parties are more likely to have guests who abide by the strict dress code. Getting everyone to go along with the dress code is much harder at a larger event.

- ✔ **Is your party celebrating a special holiday or an intimate celebration?** "Christmas in July" offers numerous theme ideas.

Bowling's not for everyone

JAYMZ SAYZ

I've thrown dozens of parties in bowling alleys. At a party for a large film company, I had men in tuxedos and women in evening gowns bowling up a storm when the head of a bowling league approached me and asked if I would throw a similar party for them.

I agreed, figuring that if a formal event worked so well in a bowling alley, it should work for a bowling league. Wrong! Some of the people tried. They wore polyester safari suits and seersucker suits, and one Jackie Gleason look-a-like wore a three-piece suit. I should have made the theme Americana, Hawaiian, or '50s. The Elegant Soiree was the wrong theme to pick — as the guests either did not have the wardrobe or misunderstood the theme.

▶ **Will your party be held in conjunction with any other event?** No point in having a costume party before going out to a movie.

▶ **Does a certain look already work with the space?** Why fight it? Some spaces just scream "theme." Why have a '70s Theme Night in a '50s diner?

▶ **What is the age group of the guests?** Younger people may love a Rubik's Cube cocktail party, while older guests would likely prefer a Spy or Brazilian theme.

▶ **What time is the party? Afternoon? Night?** Evenings lend themselves to more elaborate themes. Beach Blanket Bingo parties or American Backyard Barbecues are more versatile than the Elegant and Sophisticated Soiree theme.

Small Party Theme Ideas

Your first party will most likely be a small one. But just because the size of the party is modest doesn't mean that your ambitions have to be! Any number of themes will enable you to dazzle your guests, to let them leave knowing your party had the right stuff.

The attire, drink, food, and music suggestions that accompany the themes below are just a starting point. Various recipe ideas can be found in Chapter 9. I list a few key films for certain themes, but you'll find a more detailed list in Chapter 14. I've only included a few music selections because if you want to make your party fun and exciting, you need some variety, and new CD compilations (like the Ultra-Lounge series on Capitol/EMI) are a handy helper. My cocktail CD favorites can be found in Chapter 7 and in the appendix. Drink recipes can be found in Chapter 8.

Before-and-after

This one ties in with a special activity — an opera or a museum opening, for example. Everyone congregates at your place for a snack and drinks before heading off. Afterward, they return for more drinks and to finish off the snacks (and sometimes stay for a meal).

✔ **Attire:** Semi-formal to formal. Guests are almost always dressed for the other event, be it a night at the theater or a lecture.

✔ **Drinks:** Be careful not to let your guests get intoxicated if you are doing anything too physical. You are legally responsible for your guests if you host an event and have alcohol. For this reason I recommend Bloody Caesars and Bloody Marys over martinis. Gimlets, screwdrivers, and premix Collins would be a tasty addition. Having one drink before going out and a couple when you get back makes for a responsible and memorable evening.

✔ **Food:** Serve several hors d'oeuvres with the Before drinks, as you'll likely require energy for the event before dinner. You may consider setting up a buffet table with cold food arranged on platters. As for the dinner, think ahead so that it's basically prepared and can be quickly heated up. When I say "dinner," I don't necessarily mean a full-blown meal, but something more substantial than tiny treats.

✔ **Music:** During the Before part of your party, warm your guests up with Cab Calloway, Spike Jones, and Glenn Miller. At the After portion of your party, delight your guests with the likes of Burt Bacharach, Dick Hyman, and Enoch Light.

Christmas cocktail party

More cocktail parties take place during the winter holidays than any other time of the year. And why not? Baby, it's cold outside! You've been out in the snow, maybe out shopping. Whatever the case, the basic essentials of this one are a roaring fire in the hearth and someone playing sing-along music on the guitar or piano.

This theme has its limitations on people who don't have snow in the winter season. Of course in warm climates, trying this theme may be a kooky idea — similar to a Christmas in July party. Use your imagination around the basic Christmas themes.

Red and green are the traditional colors, and evergreen boughs or pine incense give your party the right scent for Christmas. Oh, and don't forget the mistletoe!

✔ **Attire:** You can't go wrong with green, red, and white. Silver and gold accessories go great! Sweaters or blazers for men and comfortable, warm dresses for the ladies.

✔ **Drinks:** You want hot drinks like Café Royale, Gluehwein, Hot Buttered Rum, toddies, and Tom & Jerrys.

✔ **Food:** Holiday desserts like Candied Orange Slices.

✔ **Music:** Music to consider includes Jaymz Bee and the Royal Jelly Orchestra, Bing Crosby, Ella Fitzgerald, Burl Ives, and Frank Sinatra. *Note:* Playing hymns or *A Very Yanni Christmas* may put your guests to sleep! Make sure that the selections are swingin'!

Movies to inspire

✔ *A Charlie Brown Christmas*

✔ *The Grinch Who Stole Christmas*

✔ *Rudolph the Red Nosed Reindeer* — my personal favorite — featuring the lovable Burl Ives as the voice of Sam the Snowman!

✔ *White Christmas*

Trees with all the trimmings

Decorating the Christmas tree is a good chance for you to use your imagination. If you want to do something wild, try a black light tree. Cut different shapes out of fluorescent paper and put one or two 4-foot black lights at the bottom of the tree. Watch it glow.

At one Christmas event, I had a dozen small (2-foot-high) fake Christmas trees and broke the crowd into bunches of four or five per tree. They were asked to decorate the tree using only things in their pockets and purses or clothing/jewelry. The best tree came from a group where a lovely, older woman donated her pearl necklace and used a large broach as the star on top. Cuff links, earrings, and coins covered the tree. (Of course everyone got his or her stuff back after a few photos.)

Mardi Gras, Fat Tuesday, or Carnival

Soon after Christmas, the people of southern Louisiana begin their celebration of Carnival, a marvelous explosion of four to eight weeks of parades and parties that reach their climax on Mardi Gras, a Tuesday exactly forty-six days before Easter.

For fun, use water pistols loaded with perfumed water. Have confetti and paper streamers on hand. You can throw out strings of cheap beads and chocolate doubloons.

 ✔ **Attire:** Mardi Gras celebrations are based on south-of-the-equator culture and traditionally take place before Lent and Easter in late February or early March. Lavish costuming is appropriate and expected. You can expect to see women wearing everything from ostrich plume headdresses, to Victorian gowns and crowns to Arabian nights gowns and elaborate masks.

 ✔ **Drinks:** Coffee and coconut-based rum.

 ✔ **Food:** Anything with shrimp.

 ✔ **Music:** Anything goes — but make sure that you can dance to it! If in doubt, try samba or bossa nova. (See Chapter 7 and the appendix for cocktail party music suggestions.)

He as she and she as he

This type of theme party works best for couples who are open to gender-bender experimentation. It's certainly not for everyone. You must make sure that everybody invited will follow the theme. You may wish to remind your guests that "real men" from Milton Berle to Patrick Swayze have donned drag.

 ✔ **Attire:** Men must allow their dates to dress them. (Don't leave it up to a novice to pick a dress or the right shade of lipstick.) Of course, some men will insist on keeping their beards and doing their own makeup, but that just adds to the hilarity. Women should wear men's suits.

 ✔ **Drinks:** Men get umbrellas in their drinks. Pink Ladies, Grasshoppers, and colorful martinis (blue curacao, galliano, and so on should be used for coloring) will get the role-playing under way.

Women drink from highball glasses. Scotch and soda, rye and ginger, or anything amber to dark will add to their manly posing.

✔ **Food:** Toasted herbed nuts, warm breadsticks.

✔ **Music:** There's nothing like torch songs to get things started (try Shirley Bassey, Peggy Lee, or Judy Garland), but you'll need the romantics (Frank Sinatra, Tony Bennett, or Mel Torme) to get the late feeders out of the salad bar!

Bring your own babe

Another variation of this theme is the Babes Only Bash. That is an event where women come as they are and men must dress as women to get in!

The only way this party works is if the dress code applies to absolutely everybody. Like going to a nudist colony and finding a couple of men fully dressed and gawking, it's just not proper otherwise!

Women can often get their male friends or husbands to try on a dress in private, but convincing them that going out that way is a good idea takes a little more effort. I've only done a small version of this theme, but I plan to do a three-hour boat cruise with this "babe only" criteria and can't wait to see the results, despite the fact that I look like Peg Bundy from the TV show *Married With Children* when I wear a wig!

New Year's Eve

The thing about New Year's Eve is that everyone goes out. Many of the people going out don't usually party, which makes it a tough night for club bouncers and staff. Another thing about New Year's Eve is that people have heightened expectations of fun. They need to be made to feel like they're at *the* place — right where the most action is. Regardless of your best efforts, there are so many different New Year's Eve parties that guests will be on the move making the rounds.

The traditional New Year's Eve cocktail party is in the early evening as the first stop to warm up for the long night of festivities. I suggest — unless you have a huge budget and the desire to let party planning take over your life for a couple months — that you forego the all-night party and go for a small, early cocktail party so well-done that your guests talk about it at all of their other stops.

- ✔ **Attire:** The good news with a New Year's Eve party is that everyone dresses up. While you don't want a penguinfest, you certainly need a strict dress code. Formal cocktail attire.

- ✔ **Drinks:** Champagne and a full martini menu. Make sure to have lots of smart drinks on hand for designated drivers!

- ✔ **Food:** Because New Year's Eve parties are really parties before the big party, you probably want to go all out with the best canapés you can afford, to leave your guests with a lasting impression. Also, have filling treats — chips and breadsticks — around, in case your guests won't have time for a proper meal before further partying.

- ✔ **Music:** Fast and groovy. Up-tempo mambo, cha cha, and loungecore.

Housewarming

A housewarming is simply a party to welcome someone into their new home, so every guest needs to bring a gift, even if that gift is only a refrigerator magnet. An old-fashioned open house luncheon or brunch works well, with simple finger food that requires no knives or forks. Having a housewarming doesn't mean that you have to fill your sink with dirty dishes. You're better off to go with simple treats that aren't likely to make a mess. Of course you'll have kitchen utensils handy if they're requested — if not, your housewarming party is a little prematurely timed. If your place is an empty room full of boxes, then you should try a surrealist theme.

- ✔ **Attire:** Cocktail casual: semi-formal. (Comfortable guests make for a comfy new home setting!)

- ✔ **Drinks:** Go for the old standard drinks like the highball, screwdriver, martini, Manhattan, or Fruit Cup Punch. You should always have mocktail options available, too.

✔ **Food:** Anything that can be carried in, carried out, and cleaned up quickly. "Mini" things, like mini egg rolls, are good candidates.

✔ **Music:** Something that your new neighbor can't object to. Ella Fitzgerald, Tony Bennett — keep to the crooners and swing in your new digs.

TV night

The occasion is a playoff game, election night, or an awards show. You want to show off that 38-inch television you just purchased. You don't have to worry too much about decorating or entertainment; everyone's eyes will be on that glowing screen. Just make sure that you have enough comfortable seating so everyone has a good view. You want ashtrays and places to set down glasses.

Liven up the action by making a betting pool on the event prior to start time. Have some appropriate prizes for the winners.

✔ **Attire:** It all depends what you're watching. If it's a sporting event, you may like the Bahama shirt and shorts look, but for a film, live music video, or awards show telecast, why not go for "Loungerie." Men in smoking jackets with dickies and women in glamorous (but not too revealing) evening wear. You should be certain that the people you invite will feel comfortable dressing in a theme to watch TV; otherwise just keep it casual.

✔ **Drinks:** Highballs or Screwdrivers. (I never condone "coolers.") Depending on how stubborn your friends are, you may have to supply beer for this theme.

✔ **Food:** Dip and buffalo wings. You could serve brownies that have icing numbers to make them look like TV remotes. When serving, TV trays work well if you have them.

✔ **Music:** Why not get a compilation recording (such as the TeeVee Toon series on compact disc) and air it during the TV commercial breaks? Also the "Golden Throats" series on Rhino Records is a sure-fire hit with your guests. I mean, who can resist William Shatner's version of *Mr. Tambourine Man*?

TV game show

If you are just channel surfing, waiting for the show to start, you can always play Channel Surfing Control Freak. You'll need several remotes, so you may even have to borrow some. You put six or so in a large bucket or basket and allow your guests to reach in and grab one. Whoever gets the remote control that works gets to pick the station. When someone in the group disagrees, he declares "mutiny." If a majority agree, all the remotes are placed in the bucket and the game begins again.

Valentine's Day

Valentine's Day is usually geared towards couples, so if you put on a Valentine's Day party, make sure that you think about your single friends and how to get them to attend without a Valentine. Letting them know that you're gearing the party towards singles may work, but — if that's your angle — try and come through with plenty of single people so they don't feel left out.

If you're going conventional, you want red and white colors, with some pink thrown in occasionally. Red flowers, candy hearts, and cupids are the obvious thing. You can create a real pink look to your party room with plenty of dry ice in the punch bowl and pink lights shining on it. Lace paper doilies and red and pink crepe paper would be the expected, but when you throw a party, try to spend some time on brainstorming creative surprises. Don't just run out and buy a bunch of store decorations. If you do, chances are that you'll have spent quite a bit of money and not given your guests anything to really talk about. The unique ideas are the ones that they're going to talk about.

You'll also want plenty of candles and little corners dimly lit where people can sneak away to cuddle once in a while. If you are doing a private event, I suggest that you start it about 8 p.m. and finish by 11 p.m. It's nice to have a private dinner with your sweetie, go to a small gathering, and then head home for snookums. Of course if you're single, this time frame works well too, because if you don't find the man or woman of your dreams, you still have a few hours to hit the nightclubs and bars.

> ✔ **Attire:** What you wear has to make you feel sexy. Smoking jacket or tuxedo, satin dress or PVC skirt, the main thing is that you match well with your date. Find out what your date is wearing before you commit. Red and white need not be the theme for attire. Of course, I've noticed that people from countries with a red and white flag (Canada, Japan, and Switzerland) tend to have more red and white items of clothing in their wardrobe. Valentine's Day and Canada Day cocktail parties look surprisingly alike.

> ✔ **Drinks:** Champagne, red and white wine, tropical rum punch, martinis, and plenty of juice and mineral water.

> ✔ **Food:** Tomato, Red Onion, and Roasted Yellow Bell Pepper Flatbread. Shape the flatbread like hearts.

> ✔ **Music:** Engelbert Humperdinck, Barry White, and Tom Jones of course, but dozens of great "Music for Lovers"-type compilation records are available, too. Also, you can never go wrong with Exotica.

I remember a great party. It was called "Lovers Lanes" and was an evening of candlelight bowling. The guests came walking in on a long red carpet. Right at the door, there was a preacher (who was actually a starving stand-up comedian) who gave quick wedding vows to whoever came in together. It didn't matter if they were couples or not. Two males — whatever. It was hilarious!

Spontaneous parties

Some of the best parties aren't even planned. They just happen. Someone drops by or suggests getting together after an event.

> ✔ **Attire:** It's too late to go overboard. Keep your dress appropriate but simple. No cutoff shorts or stained shirts, but gold lamè is lame, and being too flashy makes your guests feel underdressed.

> ✔ **Drinks:** If you're not the type of person who keeps a stocked bar, you can always get away with vodka, wine, and beer. Also include tonic water, soda water, and fruit juices, and don't forget the coffee!

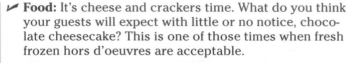

✔ **Food:** It's cheese and crackers time. What do you think your guests will expect with little or no notice, chocolate cheesecake? This is one of those times when fresh frozen hors d'oeuvres are acceptable.

If you have any vegetarian friends, make sure that you look carefully at the ingredients labels on any frozen hors d'oeuvres you've got stashed away.

✔ **Music:** Lounge and cocktail compilation CDs are the answer. They're exciting and keep the battle for the stereo demons at bay. People who always want to change the music will have no choice because the album is a compilation of various artists, and how can they complain about an artist they haven't heard yet?

If you enjoy hosting, and want to be prepared for such an event, then you're going to have to think ahead and have some basic emergency party supplies stashed away — kind of like having all of your camping gear in one place or being prepared in the event of a tornado.

Find a place in your cupboard for these items so that you can set an attractive table in no time at all. Quick is what you want to be in a spontaneous moment. After all, you don't want your guests to think that you're going to a whole lot of trouble.

Useful items to stash include:

✔ Inexpensive but attractive glassware

✔ Paper placemats and coasters

✔ A tablecloth that you keep for this purpose, or some paper ones

✔ Cocktail napkins

✔ A simple decorative table centerpiece — be it plastic flowers or a big bowl of fruit, real or plastic

✔ Candles and candlesticks

✔ A couple of bottles of liquor and mixer

✔ Some simple frozen hors d'oeuvres

✔ The ingredients for one quick dessert

The Office Cocktail Party

Partying while you work is not a good idea, but partying at work is occasionally a very good idea, particularly if your company has something, or someone, to celebrate. This section looks at two types of office parties — the celebration party and the annual holiday party — and offers some guidelines for each.

The business and office party

Maybe you are taking on the task of organizing a formal office party. These parties usually mark an occasion of some sort — paying tribute to a retiring worker or celebrating a birthday or the signing of a new contract. The party is an "inside" party of workers who are there every day and see the ups and downs of the company. Following are some general guidelines to follow:

- ✔ The party should take place in the nicest office or area of the company or at a nearby hotel or restaurant.
- ✔ The party should be short — two hours at the most.
- ✔ Dress is whatever is appropriate for the workplace, as shown in Figure 3-1.
- ✔ The party should begin on company time, an hour before closing.
- ✔ The boss should shut the entire place down for the party in order to let everyone know that this event is important and that they are considered to be family.
- ✔ Management should break the ice by diving in or distributing the first of the drinks or food and letting people loosen up a bit from their work day.
- ✔ The party should be catered. Employees of the company should not be assigned food preparation duty.
- ✔ After the ice has been properly broken with a bit of food and drink, then the sentimental speeches can be made — short and succinct. Make the presentation of the sentimental gift, propose a toast to mark the occasion, and quickly end the party. Don't let it drag on and don't keep employees long after they're off the clock.
- ✔ Don't forget the photographer.

Figure 3-1: When the work day's done, it's time to party at the office.

I was at a major record label office party where the president of the company was the bartender. That really broke down the barriers and created a team feeling.

The office holiday party

The point of this party is to give people who work together the whole year a chance to meet each other in a holiday mood. The entire point, like any office party, is to create a sense of family among the employees. You're trying to create a situation where employees who don't get to chat with each other can meet and talk a bit.

People have many opinions about this affair, but I recommend the following:

✔ This party should always start and end on company time, with the office shut down.

✔ Decide who is to be the chairperson organizing the party, give him a budget, and let him create a committee and work on the party on business hours.

✔ Set the space up in traditional cocktail party furniture placement, creating an environment that is conducive to standing, drinking, mingling, and moving around. Avoid a seating situation where people end up locked in with the same people they already know.

✔ Go with simple hors d'oeuvres, Christmas cookies, and candy — don't get into an elaborate dinner.

✔ An office party is an annual private affair, and spouses should not be invited. By keeping it on company time, this should not be a big problem.

✔ Dancing doesn't really work at an office party because it creates a situation of breaking the people into different camps and embarrasses some because of their lack of dancing skills.

✔ Management and Type-A business types should be encouraged to give up on the "agenda" at this party. *No business talk allowed!*

✔ Company executives should make the rounds, greeting as many of the employees as possible and wishing them a Merry Christmas. After that's done, they should disappear and let the employees have some fun and drinks on company expense without the boss around.

✔ Give a bonus to the office cleaning staff.

✔ Attire should probably be office casual. You can obviously loosen that tie a little, or dress up a bit for that day, but nothing too formal.

✔ Punch and spritzers are good drink choices. (You don't want anyone getting too tipsy at the office.)

✔ The party should be catered. Always.

✔ As for music, why not try Combustible Edison, Mike Flowers, Frank Bennett, Squirrel Nut Zippers, or The Royal Jelly Orchestra? Playing modern cocktail music at office parties can spark conversation and keep the mood happy.

The Christmas party
that laid an egg

I once threw a party for a company with a large budget who claimed they were "Computer Headhunters." I booked a large art gallery and had a band play during cocktail hour. The guests were then shown into a large open space for dinner and dancing. Before they finished their meal, a comedian stood up to perform. I had warned the party chairman that comedy is risky at these types of events, but he insisted.

I thought that the comedian was very funny and quite charming. Apparently, someone didn't agree with me. A very intoxicated woman rushed the stage and began heckling the comedian. He was at a disadvantage. At a comedy club he could use an offensive comeback — but here he was concerned about not offending guests at a private party.

This woman would not let up until a few co-workers walked her back to her table. The comedian finished with one very quick joke and flew off the stage. The president of the company offered his apologies. The next morning he fired the heckler.

The obvious lesson: Don't get drunk at an office party — ever!

Chapter 4
Themes for Large Parties

In This Chapter

▶ Celebrating the past

▶ Cavorting in the tropics

▶ Dressing up

▶ Dressing like Bond — or not

▶ Dressing in a sheet

*L*arge theme parties are the essence of old Technicolor movies or tinted vacation brochures — what you'd really like to believe you'd see in a foreign locale or on a holiday. When I say *theme,* I'm talking about boiling it down to the basic broad cultural stereotype, the idealized version of that country. The types of images you find in travelogue films and 3-D exotic Viewmaster slides.

So, say you're going to do a Tacky Tourist party. The guys would dress in unmatched polyester with a camera around the neck, a large plastic shopping bag, and perhaps a straw hat. The host must decide on what the basic party essence is and stay true to it in everything from color and decorations to music and hors d'oeuvres. But a good theme actually makes coordinating all of those elements easier, because it gives you a focus!

If you need general tips on selecting a theme, check out Chapter 3. Just as in Chapter 3, the theme suggestions in this chapter include ideas for attire, drinks, food, and music. Some of the drink recipes I mention here are covered in Chapter 8; some of the food recipes in Chapter 9. For even more information, turn to *Bartending For Dummies* by Ray Foley, *Cooking For Dummies* by Bryan Miller and Marie Rama, *Lowfat Cooking For Dummies* by Lynn Fischer, and *Gourmet Cooking For Dummies* by Charlie Trotter, all published by IDG Books Worldwide, Inc. For more on party music, check out Chapter 7 and the appendix.

Americana Backyard Barbecue

This theme party has the Ward Cleaver and Ozzie Nelson family standard to aspire to. It celebrates an era of the 1950s when a middle-class family with a single wage earner could still afford a house, a car, all the latest household appliances, and an annual vacation with their two and a half children.

If you have a large space with hardwood floors, then maybe you can have waiters and waitresses on roller skates.

> ✔ **Attire:** In hot weather, you'll want to keep your guests comfy and allow them to wear summer dresses and suits, as shown in Figure 4-1. You may even allow bowling shirts if the sun hasn't set yet.

Figure 4-1: This couple's ready to rock around the clock — or until the party is over.

- **Drinks:** Mint juleps, gin and tonic, and fruit punch.
- **Food:** For the daring, try Beef and Turkey Meat Loaf. If that sounds too strange, join me in some simple white-bread American mini-sandwiches.
- **Music:** Try Perry Como, The Hi Los, or Lambert Hendricks and Ross.

Movies to inspire:

- *Edward Scissorhands*
- *Hairspray*
- *American Graffiti*

Block shots

JAYMZ SAYZ The Americana Backyard Barbecue is a good party for "block shots." You get somebody with a flatbed truck to pick up a huge 5 foot by 3 foot block of ice at an ice supply house. Ask the ice house to saw or create a small waterfall-like ramp from one end of the ice to the other. Place the ice in the back of the pickup truck with the lower end of the ramp near the very back of the truck. Up on the truck bed, near the high end of the ice ramp, have a bartender ready, bottle and shot glass in hand. Guests can come up and place their open mouths near the end of the ice ramp. The bartender pours a shot onto the top of the ramp, and by the time it hits the mouth, it's been properly chilled.

Beach Blanket Bingo

Beach Blanket Bingo is the beach party of Frankie Avalon and Annette Funicello beach movies: the Sea-esta by the sea. The look is beach blankets, suntans, surfboards, skate-boards, bodysurfing, beach balls, and binoculars. Surfin' all day and swingin' all night.

If the moon and the waves are calling you, haul in some sand, grab a beach blanket made for two, and get away from the crowd for a while. You'll be dancing the Frug, the Swim, and the Twist.

✔ **Attire:** The clothes (or lack of them) are bikinis, hip-huggers, toreadors, and cashmere sweaters with pumps for the beach bunnies. For the lads it's swimsuits, knee-high cutoffs, beachcomber hats, and gold neckchains. Of course East Indian fashion can create an interesting variation. I love to wear my white silk Punjabi pajamas to the beach.

A couple of hired dancers (possibly in highly reflective bathing suits, like in Elvis Presley's *Clambake*) can really make this party come alive.

✔ **Drinks:** Plenty of water and juice! If you bring alcohol and it is not a private beach, you could be in for trouble. If you have a permit for alcohol, a little tequila goes a long way!

✔ **Food:** Rolled pinwheel sandwiches belong at any outdoor event. Handmade potato chips are worth the effort. Also, you can cut fresh vegetables up beforehand and put them on a tray with some dip.

✔ **Music:** The B52s, The Beach Boys, Shadowy Men From A Shadowy Planet, and the Ventures are all good choices. Plenty of surf music is available on CD reissues, but if you want to make it more interesting, bring plenty of cocktail compilation CDs for your portable blaster. Mambo, exotic, and jazz all fit in after dusk. Live entertainers work very well at this party. The emcee should encourage people to sing TV themes, Cole Porter classics, and so on, leaving the folk songs for the happy campers at the other end of the beach.

Movies to inspire:

✔ *Beach Blanket Bingo*

✔ *Beach Party*

✔ *Muscle Beach Party*

Caribbean

When I talk about the Caribbean islands, I'm talking about approximately thirty inhabited islands and over seven hundred uninhabited islands in the West Indies south and southeast of Florida. These include Haiti, Jamaica, Trinidad,

Grenada, and Guadeloupe. These islands are inhabited by many different races and have varying traditions, but for the sake of a theme party, I'm going to go for the broad cultural stereotype: white sand, tropical flowers, birds, shells, fish netting, real grass in various colors, and grass mats. Bamboo stools and a few hammocks should be supplied for your tired guests, who have spent hours dancing to the exotic rhythms, romantic melodies, and intriguing sounds.

- ✔ **Attire:** Less is more. Bikinis, Bahamas shirts, and shorts.

- ✔ **Drinks:** Drinks can include Rum Swizzle, Mai Tai, daiquiri, fruit cup punch, Collins, Morgan Punch, Hazel's Pick-Me-Up, and Mariner's Grog. The traditional cocktail in parts of the Caribbean is gin in coconut milk, but rum has always been a favorite, too.

- ✔ **Food:** Banana meringue is a traditional island desert. Whatever your offerings, set your food out on a long, low, green-strewn table. Arrange the food and add color and ambiance to the display with flowers, fruit, coconuts, bananas, and mango. You may wish to serve a salt cod dip or go for Braised Spare Ribs with Honey and Chipotte Peppers.

- ✔ **Music:** The traditional music is rumba, reggae, steel drum bands, salsa, or calypso. I suggest listening to Harry Belafonte, the Merrymen, or Mighty Sparrow. For added fun you can have a limbo contest using a length of rope or a bamboo pole. How low can you go?

Costume Party

A masquerade party can be a whole lot of fun, especially if people are dressed up beyond recognition. Perhaps you can re-enact a Victorian ballroom scene. While couples waltz around an elegant ballroom to the music of a string quartet, others flirt and mingle from behind the cover of their petite, hand-held masks.

Halloween and Festnacht are the most common dress-up parties. Festnacht is a lot like Halloween except that it is held in early March and lasts between three days and a week.

People dress in eerie clown costumes and play marching music down the streets at all hours of the day. The strangest celebration I've seen occurs in Basel, Switzerland. All the lights of the city are turned off and thousands of costumed Swiss play music with lanterns on their heads! You'll find that if you can get people to wear a costume, that alone automatically puts them in the right mood for a party.

Halloween is a huge adult party night, second only to New Year's Eve. What that means is that you either need to really go all out in order to be the best, or just do an early two-hour "pre-other party" stop that everyone talks about the rest of the night.

- ✔ **Attire:** No costume — no entry.

- ✔ **Drinks:** Vodka and juice means you can sip through a straw, and that means less glass washing for you and less make-up smear for them. Punch is usually recommended, but should always be served by someone other than a guest.

- ✔ **Food:** Oysters on the Half Shell; Roasted Garlic Puree.

- ✔ **Music:** "The Monster Mash," the themes from *The Munsters* or *The Addams Family,* and the *Rocky Horror Picture Show* soundtrack are all staples, but any high-energy music from Yello or Ryuichi Sakamoto would be a welcome twist.

Mixed up music

JAYMZ SAYZ I remember parties my friend Hugo would throw at his little cafe in Switzerland.

He always threw a Festnacht party after parading through a nearby village. He put Frank Sinatra, Tony Bennett, and Dean Martin singles in the jukebox. The trick is, he never changed the cards in the machine, so when customers paid to hear Led Zepplin's "Stairway To Heaven," they would get Bobby Darren's "Mack The Knife." The party was so wild and the music was so great that nobody seemed to complain or notice.

The Elegant and Sophisticated Soiree

This party is high-class and upscale, with the finest dress, decor, and hors d'oeuvres. I'm talking about the classic cocktail party of the movies: elegantly dressed people mingling in a chandelier ballroom while a pianist plays sentimental tunes in the background. Excuse me for a moment while I sigh.

This particular party takes some money to do right, as this kind of class doesn't come cheap. If you decide to take on this theme, then you must go all out in glassware, drinks, and the best food.

A large party rental outlet (the kind that does weddings and such) will rent you centerpieces, table covers, table skirts, and covers in every color. White votive candles can work very well. They add an element of romance, as long as they are good quality.

Cheap candles burn unevenly, making them less attractive and potentially dangerous. Candle "sculptures" are another fire hazard. A sailboat or poodle candle is meant as an art piece — they usually burn very poorly and only look good lit for the first half hour. (My house burnt to the ground in 1981 after a roommate left a poodle candle lit overnight.)

> ✔ **Attire:** Ladies, if you're dreaming about this one, first imagine if you have any chance of getting the guys on your invitation list to attend wearing bow ties, cummerbunds, and cuff links. If not, you may be spending a great deal of money and time to only end up feeling a bit disappointed.
>
> One variation on this theme is to throw a 1920s party, when only the best-dressed couples were admitted to the best speakeasies, as shown in Figure 4-2. Still elegant, but fun.
>
> ✔ **Drinks:** Champagne and martinis. If you must serve beer, at least don't let anyone walk around with beer in a can or bottle. If going beerless won't be a major inconvenience for your guests, this theme works better without beer.

Figure 4-2: Formal attire was needed for this flapper and her date to get admitted.

✔ **Food:** Spiced Shrimp or Olive and Pecorino Cheese Tapenade on Toasted French Bread.

✔ **Music:** Tony Bennett, Xavier Cugat, or Frank Sinatra.

Retro ('50s, '60s, '70s, '80s) Party

People love retro, and most won't be scrutinizing your every ashtray to see if you've kept to your theme. However, the more you do, the better the subliminal effect will be. As long as you play music that was made during your chosen decade(s), and you ask people to dress for the theme, you'll have a great time. No one will nit-pick about whether or not your guests are wearing shoes from the '50s or '70s.

1950s

This party pays homage to the glory days of the cocktail party. It's a throwback to a postwar time — '46 to '65 —

when America was the top country and everything seemed very secure. It's not just the music and the dress — the sociological aspect is tied in as well.

Your party should be like walking into a '50s bar and finding Dean Martin and Sammy Davis, Jr. sipping martinis. Your tailored tux is still warm from the valet's iron, with the pocket handkerchief folded all nice. A bit of a vest is peeking out from under your tux coat.

This party is Lake Tahoe's South Shore or New York's Copacabana, or the Casbar Lounge of the Hotel Sahara in Vegas. Your party is filled with the peculiar air that successful clubs have: a combination of cigarette smoke, overheated air, and cleaned linen.

Parties in this era were kind of a guys' world. But the women who could hang in that world — be it Angie Dickinson or Shirley MacLaine — were strong women who could party with the best of them. And it wasn't as if the girls were being exploited; they were having as much fun as the guys.

A dark-colored, traditional-looking lounge look works well. If you're going '50s, Japanese lanterns can work, too.

- ✔ **Attire:** Men should be in suit jackets and thin ties. For ladies that don't want to wear a cocktail dress, then Toreador pants can work. They're the waist-to-ankle, snug leggings that were popularized in the late '50s and early '60s. They can be worn with stiletto heels or with flats, toes both pointed and round. They work well in almost all colors, but need to be ankle-length or just above and nice and tight.

- ✔ **Drinks:** Punch or anything in an old-fashioned glass (Scotch, Rye and Ice, and so on).

- ✔ **Food:** The 1950s were a decade of convenience. Cubes of cheese and Spam typify the processed food of the era.

  One of the more unusual parties I went to was called "Spamhenge." The hosts had a 1950s theme, but re-created Stonehenge with processed meat. Although few guests partook, we still haven't stopped talking about it. Who knows? Had they carved Easter Island heads out of Spam, it may have gone over better!

- ✔ **Music:** Your guests should listen to Frank Sinatra, Tony Bennett, Louis Prima with Keely Smith, or Dean Martin.

Movies to inspire:

- *Breakfast at Tiffany's*
- *Kiss Me, Stupid*
- *Sweet Smell of Success*
- *Hairspray*
- *Teacher's Pet*

1960s

If you want to do early '60s, maybe you're talking about a hullabaloo, swinging sixties, pre-psychedelia kind of look — a combination of Carnaby street and Mod.

- **Attire:** Several different looks were popular in the decade, including what I'd call the "Formal Hippie" look illustrated in Figure 4-3. Guys were doing the Mod look; gals were wearing wraparounds or cocktail miniskirts with go-go boots. A pea coat or a maxi coat can mix well with a miniskirt. If you're going with a sweater, then one that's beaded at the neckline will work the best.

- **Drinks:** Tall drinks with umbrellas and fruit made a strong showing in the decade. Try zombies and Bloody Caesars.

- **Food:** Communal food — things that everyone can share. Try vegetables and dip, or anything vegetarian.

- **Music:** Movie soundtracks — everything from any James Bond film to any spy movie track to *The Party* — are appropriate. Light psychedelia, typified by Strawberry Alarm Clock, was also popular.

Movies to inspire

- *Beyond the Valley of the Dolls*
- *Casino Royale*
- *The Nutty Professor* (the 1963 version)
- *The Party*

That theme she does

JAYMZ SAYZ I've recorded a couple of CDs with the Royal Jelly Orchestra. We also do parties. One of the biggest we've performed at was a bash during the Toronto International Film Festival for actor Tom Hanks and his film *That Thing You Do.*

One of Canada's leading party consultants, "Party Barbara Hershenhorn," went a little theme-crazy on the snacks — macaroni and cheese and hot dogs! This fit with the theme of the movie, but some of the guests had come in tuxedos expecting fine cuisine, not "common" food.

Nonetheless, you could tell by how few complained that the party was a great success, because Barbara spared no expense in going for her theme. Everybody left knowing they were at a happening.

Figure 4-3: Mr. Mod and his peace-loving date are perfect for a '60s bash.

1970s

The late '70s are best captured in *Can't Stop The Music,* the wonderfully awful disco-era film starring those macho men, the Village People. Another great inspiration: television's *The Love Boat.*

> ✔ **Attire:** If you go with the disco theme, encourage your guests (male and female) to arrive in costume as the Village People — a biker, a traffic cop, a Native American, a construction worker, or a cowboy. You may even want to hand out cardboard handlebar mustaches for all the guests to wear. If you don't want your guests to dress up like the Village People, then go disco. Can you say polyester? Can you say leisure suit? Can you say gold chains?
>
> If you go with television, polyester is still the norm, as shown in Figure 4-4. *Love Boat* guests can compete for the best Captain Steubing outfit; don't forget Gopher and Julie, your cruise director!
>
> ✔ **Drinks:** Go for mixed drinks like rum and Coke that were big with the bar set of the '70s. Don't forget the Tequila Sunrise. Sure, the song about it wasn't disco, but that can't be helped.
>
> ✔ **Food:** Fresh-frozen hors d'oeuvres seem very appropriate for such a fake decade.
>
> ✔ **Music:** Make sure that you have lots of extended play versions of "Disco Inferno," "Love Hangover," "Born To Be Alive," "I Feel Love" — and of course anything and everything by the Village People. To accentuate your *Love Boat* night, you've got to have the theme song by Jack Jones. Charo also has a cover of the song.

1980s

Truth be told, the cocktail movement wouldn't be undergoing a resurgence today if there hadn't been so few cocktail parties thrown during the '80s. In other words, this decade was the cocktail dark ages. That makes this a difficult — but not impossible — era to replicate.

Figure 4-4: Just love that '70s polyester!

- ✔ **Attire:** Kid Creole and the Coconuts, Joe Jackson, and Bryan Ferry were the only cocktail trendsetters of the era. As you can see from Figure 4-5, the closest thing to cocktail chic in the decade was the New Romantic look (yeech!).

- ✔ **Drinks:** The clothes weren't the only thing with a feminine angle. The booze was watered down, too. Shooters (anything that can be popped in one gulp, preferably something sweet) and spritzers were the norm.

- ✔ **Food:** Given the "Me" theme of the decade, you don't want things that are shared with others — casseroles and such. You want individual servings, as with Garlic and Goat Cheese Tartines.

- ✔ **Music:** Again, anything by Kid Creole, Ferry, and Jackson. That other famous musical Jackson — Michael — definitely is not cocktail.

Figure 4-5: The '80s had few fashion inspirations for cocktail parties.

Rubik's Cube Cocktail Party

A friend of mine read about this on the Internet, and we had to try it. What a blast! The invitations were color photocopied and had a picture of a Rubik's Cube with the pertinent information. The details were pretty well followed.

The party rules:

- ✔ You must wear solid colors to the party, and only colors that are on the Cube (consult photo).
- ✔ You must wear at least three different solid colors.
- ✔ After you have arrived at the party, you must exchange your clothes with others. Everybody is trying to leave the party dressed in a solid color.

The outcome is hilarious when your guests are all different sizes!

✔ **Attire:** Be sure that the solid colors you wear are the same shade found on a Rubik's cube.

✔ **Drinks:** Many new "thirst-quenching beverages" are on the market in bright, vibrant colors. Try adding a splash of flavored vodka. So many combinations!

✔ **Food:** Cubed Eggs, anything else in cubes.

✔ **Music:** Music for squares? Nah! Throw on some cocktail compilation CDs!

Science

I've seen two good variations of this theme. One is a Sputnik '50s–'60s space kitsch. Think *Lost in Space* and *Star Trek,* moon rocks and space rubble, and lunar terrain vehicles. You want astronauts standing on the launch pad, drinking colored drinks. The other variation celebrates the future and the better life that scientific improvements can offer.

Pick up a couple of lava lamps, and don't forget the dry ice.

✔ **Attire:** White for the "retro science" party. Anything white. For the futuristic science party, try something like Figure 4-6.

✔ **Drinks:** Serve exotic drinks that look like they ought to be gurgling around in a test tube.

✔ **Food:** Test Tube Chilled Soup.

✔ **Music:** Juan Esquivel. Enoch Light. Anyone who used stereo panning with wild joyous abandon. (*Panning* is moving sound from left to right on your speaker — it's done in degrees these days, but when it first became available, producers went gaga over it.)

Figure 4-6: This couple is ready to step out — or guest star on *The Jetsons.*

Science down under

JAYMZ SAYZ

To give you an idea of how far you can go in decorating to a theme, let me tell you about one of the best-looking bars I've ever seen, a place in Australia called The Test Tube Factory.

The club was lit in low blacklight and was a weird cross between pop culture and science. The walls were painted with huge murals of Marilyn Monroe, James Dean, the Kennedys, Einstein, and Frankenstein.

Behind the bar — instead of hardwood and mirrors — was a huge, convoluted labyrinth of gurgling glassware: beakers, retorts, valves, test tubes, and surgical tubing. Beautifully designed and meshed together, this gurgling maze pumped and frothed in green and pink fluorescent liquids.

The barmaids wore purple medical short skirts with red crosses and big stethoscopes. They carried cigarette girl-style test tube trays lit up with small blacklights; the trays were fully loaded with glowing shooter drinks in big syringes. When you purchased a drink, the barmaid placed the 20 cc syringe into your mouth and squirted the drink right in.

Another great science bar was The Glowing Pickle located in Berlin. It was decorated wall-to-wall with old East German computers. The bartenders donned lab coats and served beverages in test tubes under a black light. Every night at midnight they would electrify a dill pickle. While it was frying inside it would glow and give off a pleasant yet strange odor. The club attracted some of the most interesting artists in Berlin, even though they never advertised!

South of the Border

This theme plays on the broad cultural stereotype of Mexico. Warm weather and miracle candles. Guests serenaded by a strolling guitar player with lilting, dreamy reveries. You can create the look with fake chili peppers (both red and green), fake cherries, fruit, and avocados. Luminaria, candles placed upright in the sand inside paper bags, or tall wrought-iron candlesticks with red candlesticks may be appropriate to light the walkways.

- ✔ **Attire:** Ponchos and sombreros.
- ✔ **Drinks:** Margaritas, Tequila Sunrise, Salty Dog, Fizz, Villeneuve Special, gin and tonic, and banana daiquiri will be the drinks of choice.
- ✔ **Food:** The key word here is Mexican. You'll want a lush bounty of tropical fruits and perhaps fish or shellfish.

Mexican sunflower seeds make a good munchie. Sure, you could go the easy route on food and grab a bag of chips and salsa. Don't do that. Chapter 9 has some great homemade salsa recipes. Or go for mini corn tortillas and Albondigas.

> ✔ **Music:** Treat your guests to Juan Esquivel and mariachi music.

The primary Mexican colors are red, orange, and yellow. A sombrero turned upside down and filled with fruit, green peppers, and a couple of maracas can be quite effective. Pottery and earthenware look good.

The Day of the Dead party is a variation on this theme, featuring death motifs, skull-shaped candies, and such.

Spy Party

While spy theme music blasts out of your stereo, men with slicked-back hair under hats will be sleuthing about in your bathroom looking for clues as to what prescription drugs you're taking that make you such an amiable host. But that's all right, because you have already bugged the bathroom.

> ✔ **Attire:** Men should wear trenchcoats or dress in black suits with thin black ties and a white shirt (as seen in the film *Men in Black*). Beige or brown are good too. Women can either go for the exotic foreign double agent look (imagine any female villain in a Bond movie) or the businesswoman look in a "power" suit.
>
> ✔ **Drinks:** Serve James Bond's cocktail: a medium-dry vodka martini served shaken, not stirred.

> In the early '60s, cocktail party enthusiasts made a cult of the James Bond martini, even going to great lengths to describe the dryness they required. Some people used a dry vermouth atomizer to lightly spray the glass. Other connoisseurs claimed to just pass the vermouth bottle over the martini glass.
>
> ✔ **Food:** Bouillabaisse, canapés.
>
> ✔ **Music:** Soundtracks to almost any James Bond film can be found in large record stores. Henry Mancini records are great to get you started, and spy jazz compilations like *Crime Scene* on Capitol/EMI's popular Ultra-lounge Series is best when the party is going at full speed.

Any movie starring characters such as James Bond, Matt Helm, Derek Flint, or Austin Powers will put guests in the mood of the theme.

Stag Night and Doe Night

Mixed gender is great, but sometimes getting away from the opposite sex is good, for both men and women. Still, a few hours away from your significant other is enough . . . why not have him or her join in later?

This type of party must have a venue large enough to have men only on one floor and women only on another. You can use two apartments in the same building or on the same floor of the house. The most important thing here is to have two hosts. A woman will know if her guests play cards or would be open to having a male dancer attend. Ditto applies for the men. A good men's stag night can revolve around poker, bridge, a game on TV, or just conversation. You may want to hire some exotic dancers or show adult movies — but clear it with the guest of honor first and include the information on the invitation.

✔ **Attire:** For both men and women, the idea is to cover your skin, but you want to feel a little bit wild. Fancy fabrics (silks, satins, and even leather) are the idea. As an alternative, you can dress in 1940s garb, an era when people thought they were more sophisticated than they were, as in Figure 4-7.

✔ **Drinks:** Simple bar fare works just fine for this kind of party. Go for the stereotypical men's drinks, simple and timeless. Martinis, on-the-rocks, highballs, Rickeys, mists. For the women, flavored martinis, Brandy Alexander, Pink Lady, grasshopper.

✔ **Food:** Chips, pretzels, and peanuts are all that's required.

✔ **Music:** For the does, you want Barry White, Bryan Ferry, and Lou Rawls. For the stags, Peggy Lee, Julie London, and the crooners — Frank Sinatra, Jerry Vale, and so on.

Forget about any fancy decorations. Provide plenty of large ashtrays and coasters and make the seating comfortable and the food and drink plentiful.

Figure 4-7: Ready for a night out with the boys — and the girls.

A close call with a stag

JAYMZ SAYZ

I once threw a stag party for one of my closest friends. He told me he'd like it to be a small affair of about two dozen, and that his immediate family and in-laws wouldn't be coming.

I assumed that I could let my imagination run wild with the theme. I was going to arrange a large horseshoe-shaped table. The men would sit around the outside of the table while the exotic dancers worked the space inside. Some hilarious surprises were planned, too.

The day before the bash, my friend told me his father-in-law and several cousins would be joining, and asked me to tone down whatever I'd planned.

Fortunately, I had a second place reserved in the back of my mind. It was only a few blocks from the original site and the day before the event I was lucky enough to find it available!

Instead of making twenty phone calls, I had two friends act as spies and hangout in front of the empty venue. One would stay put and keep the guests waiting while the other drove them to the party in his 1969 jet black El Toreador.

The event involved lots of card playing and a great DJ who spun classic old vinyl and played various videos (*Playboy,* the *Sports Illustrated* swimsuit TV special, clips from Fashion TV, and old episodes of the *20 Minute Workout*) on monitors around the room. Tastefully racy.

I learned two lessons on this hectic occasion. First of all, be ready with a second location and to adapt the theme accordingly (Plan B or, as I call it, The Bee Plan); and secondly, if you think your plans may offend someone or are too grandiose, you are probably right!

Hard-core pornography (XXX films) doesn't belong at cocktail parties, even if it's a stag party! Chances are that some of your guests — if not most — would feel uncomfortable or offended. Only you know the limits of your friends, but keep in mind that at a gathering of friends the point is to make your guests feel comfortable, not like party poopers!

Surrealist Party

Think Dali. Think hard. If you're one of the few lucky ones with an art background, perhaps you immediately have visions of what to do with a concept like this. For those of you who think I am going to suggest you hire a mime for a bartender, think again!

Simply put, anything really unusual goes. If most of your friends are the John and Jane Doe types, it'll take some effort in the costume department. The idea is not to go overboard, otherwise it's too much like a costume party. Instead, make your entertainment and ambiance the surreal element of your evening.

You can cover your sofa in rocks, hang shoes from the ceiling — doing things that make little or no sense is encouraged. I don't want to give too many ideas here, because I've never used the same idea twice at a Surrealist Party. Anything goes!

Films to inspire a surreal mood: *The Ten Thousand Fingers of Dr. T., The Forbidden Zone,* and most any film by Fellini or Jodorowsky.

- ✔ **Attire:** I always recommend that guests do something minimally weird, like wearing a sausage for a tie or large gloves instead of shoes. Perhaps ladies wear their dresses backwards (this doesn't work for backless gowns) or wear broccoli for earrings. Asking for "Minimal Surrealism" on your invitation's dress code will mean different things to everyone. But that's why it works.

- ✔ **Drinks:** Schnapps, grappa, and liqueurs — served in snifters or goblets that are not usually associated with these beverages. For those who don't want alcohol, make them smart drinks. Carrot juice, wheat grass juice, and other really healthy drinks usually look and taste pretty surreal. (You can also add vodka to these, making them not-so-smart drinks.)

- ✔ **Food:** Garlic and Goat Cheese Tartines, Salvador Dali Olives

- ✔ **Music:** You may wish to play two or more records at once. I've played a Mel Torme and the Meltones CD at volume 6 while playing an ambient album by Brian Eno at volume 2 or 3. Your guests might not notice for several songs. The effect is more haunting than irritating if done right. This party is also the ideal place to play 8-track tapes, if you can find a decent selection of music. You can have a DJ set up with an 8-track player, a record player, and a CD machine. Changing between these formats adds a subtle twist to the sound.

Tiki Night, or the Hawaiian/ Polynesian Theme

Fantasies of sand, sea, and sun and the swinging grass-skirts of beautiful hula girls. This theme is in the great tradition of tropical escapism, leaving the worries of the modern world behind. As the guests arrive — wearing colorful Hawaiian shirts and flowers in their hair — greet them with a kiss on both cheeks and place a lei around their neck.

The look is surfboards, Japanese lanterns, shells, Tiki torches, fish netting, real dried grass in various colors, and Lahall mats. You can buy or rent fake fruit and birds.

- ✔ **Attire:** The clothes are Hawaiian shirts, hula and grass skirts, leis, and bikini bottoms. Men wear tropical shirts and shorts.

- ✔ **Drinks:** The drinks must be tropical, too. A zombie or a Mai Tai will be thirst-quenchingly appropriate. Large glasses with swizzle sticks, umbrellas, and so on. Exotic fruit juices (passion fruit, mango, kiwi, pineapple, and so on) go well with or without rum or vodka.

- ✔ **Food:** At this party, you want to be sure and have a fruit platter of mango slices, pineapples, and coconut. Shellfish are good.

I have a friend who makes a volcano cake that explodes. If you can come up with something similar from a fancy cookbook, it will cause a rumble at this party!

- ✔ **Music:** Martin Denny, Don Ho, Yma Sumac, Arthur Lyman. This party is also an ideal occasion to hire a talented musician to serenade on ukulele or a Hawaiian lap steel.

Toga Party

The general idea here is the re-enactment of pagan Rome debauchery. Keep in mind that in Rome a man was old at 22, so I'm really talking about teenage debauchery. You want a bowl of grapes. Encourage the feeding of such to each other.

- ✔ **Attire:** Bedsheets, curtains, or any fabric you can wrap around your body will suffice. Flowers in the hair or a crown of vines enhance your simple ensemble.

I've seen toga party invitations that discouraged the wearing of underwear. Don't do this. By inviting people to a toga party, you're already pushing the limits as to their comfort level; don't push it! Always give your guests the option of wearing underwear.

- **Drinks:** Serve up screwdrivers, Collins, or Villeneuve Specials, or have a punch in a central location where the "hunters" can replenish their supply of grog or Dark n' Stormy. This is another occasion where beer may be in order.

- **Food:** Stuffed Grape Leaves, and plenty of fruit!

- **Music:** Forget the soundtrack from *Animal House* and try Gentle Giant, Momus, or any Exotica records that were recommended for the Tiki Party.

Movies to inspire:

- *Ben Hur* (based on the book that started all of the legends)

- *Satyricon*

- *Caligula*

Part III
Setting the Mood

The 5th Wave   By Rich Tennant

"The guests are getting hungry. You'd better push over another garbage dumpster."

In this part...

People get most of their information from visual or aural stimuli. "So what?" you ask. Well, pretend for a minute that you're going to a cocktail party. The invitation looked like a joke. When you show up at the door, the venue is so brightly lit that you can't help notice the cracking paint on the wall. You have to climb over two couches right by the door to get in. And the record player in the corner is playing acid rock loud enough to drown out jet planes.

In the party mood yet? I didn't think so.

Don't let this happen to you. From your invitations to your decor to your music, you want your guests to be ready to rumba (or whatever). This part shows you how.

Chapter 5
Invitations

*Y*ou know where your party is going to be. You know what your budget is and how many people you're going to invite. You know what your theme is. Now is your last chance to change your plans before you make the invitations.

If you're putting on a small and intimate party for under 20 of your friends, then you may be tempted to just pick up the phone or send an e-mail message. That may be all right for last-minute get-togethers and casual flings, but it's not all right for a cocktail party. Sure, sending out invitations is going to take a little time, effort, and expense, but that is what a well-thought-out party is all about.

Why Can't I Just Phone Again?

Remember, the invitation sets the mood for your party. When a person receives your invitation, she is going to make a snap decision as to what your party is about and whether it's worth going to. Your great invitation generates excitement and anticipation; it's a bit of foreplay that helps to put your guests in the party mood and tells them your party is one not to be missed.

Designing and sending invitations is also important for the following reasons:

> ✔ **You want your guests to dress up.** By making an invitation and setting a tone, you are visually telling the invited that you expect them to take the same care in their "look." Of course, you should state any dress code requirements on the invite as well. Phrases such as

"cocktail casual," "semi-formal," or "lounge attire encouraged" are common. As the host or hostess, you decide how strict you want your dress code to be. You can inspire your guests to dress appropriately both by the phrasing and the illustration (or letter font).

✔ **A cocktail party has a beginning and ending time.** By prominently printing the time on your invitation, people are more likely to regard it as truth, showing up on time and leaving at the designated time. A traditional cocktail party usually begins at 5 p.m. and ends at 7 p.m. Your guests are expected to show up at 5 p.m. and leave around 7 p.m. Some guests will show up late, of course, but they're still expected to leave at 7 p.m. If you really want the party to end at a certain time, then make sure that the food runs out, even if you end up with a tray left over in your refrigerator.

✔ **A cocktail party is never a dinner party — unless you state otherwise!** By having an invitation, you can make this fact more clear; people won't show up hungry and expect a full meal. At a traditional cocktail party, you want to give your guests hors d'oeuvres, but still send them away ready for dinner. If you're putting on an evening party that runs for 3 or 4 hours, that's a different situation. Some people will show up later and some will leave earlier, but the wording of your invitation lets them know what to expect.

✔ **You'll get better attendance.** People place more importance on an event that they receive an invitation for — an invitation that they can hold in their hands. People believe what they see more than what they hear.

Many people will make their attendance decision based solely on the look of the invitation. You want them to say, "Wow, this party looks very classy and exclusive! Am I ever lucky to have received this!"

✔ **An invitation is easier to remember, while a phone message may be lost or forgotten.** Some people have difficulty refusing a phone request. You may catch them unawares with a phone call; they'll say "yes" just to be polite, but then they won't actually show up at your party.

In this obligated and overbooked world, many people have short memories. You want your invitation to arrive looking like fun, not like an obligation. If someone forgets, or shows up at the wrong time, or is dressed for the beach at your Christmas party, at least you're not to blame. He received an invitation. Or maybe one of your guests won't like the fun you have planned; she can look at the invitation, consider, and politely pass.

✔ **You want to warn of any "surprises" that may offend.** You may want to tell your guests if your guest list includes press people, drag queens, lawyers, or performance artists. Let your guests know if video cameras are going to be used. Obviously, should you hire live entertainment, they will be listed as well.

By doing a nice invitation, you set a standard for yourself that you have to live up to. Your party has to be as nice as your invitation, and both are equally important. People keep great invitations, and anyone who didn't attend will see the invitation and hear about the fabulous party he missed.

Once you have earned a reputation as a party planner or cocktail host, you have reached a state of excellence that must be maintained. You cannot cut corners on your invitation (or any other detail). In fact, you can challenge yourself to come up with something even more difficult and outlandish after a while.

Okay, Okay — I'll Make an Invitation

You understand the importance of and difference that a great invitation makes for your party, and you're ready to start designing. So what goes on it?

✔ The reason for having the party

✔ Theme

✔ Date

✔ Time

✔ Dress code

✔ Address/location

✔ Bar policy (Cash bar, free bar, the first two free, and so on) Always mention if it's a cash bar or not!

An invitation is all about establishing a style; you're saying that you have great taste and that your party is going to be fun. With the availability of computer graphics and nice photocopy machines, this task is really not so formidable. But if invitation layout is something you don't feel comfortable with, then you should hire someone who can visually portray the feel that you want your party to have. If you know someone who has the artistic skill or classy handwriting to pull off your invitation, recruit her to help with the invitation.

Whatever you do, you want to be consistent to your theme. If you're doing a Tiki theme, the invitations are not just about using the word Tiki. They're about the look, the colors, and the bamboo lettering.

Figure 5-1 shows a bad invitation. The things wrong include:

✔ Crucial information missing, such as:

  • What's the date of the party?

  • What's the end time?

  • Is there an occasion being celebrated?

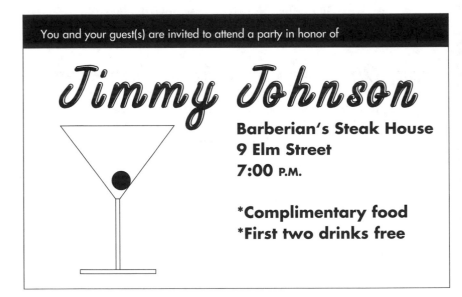

Figure 5-1: This invitation needs a little help.

- Is there a theme or dress code?
- Is the food a meal, or just hors d'oeuvres?

✔ Too many fonts. Try to keep your letter styling similar.

✔ No indication of how many people a guest may bring. "Admit one" or "You and a guest" are the norm.

✔ A dull graphic.

✔ No indication as to whether or not guests should RSVP (see "Things to keep in mind when responding to an invitation," later in this chapter, for more on RSVPs).

Figure 5-2 shows a good invitation. Some of the invitation's highlights include:

✔ A complete and accurate address. The nearest major intersection is a nice touch.

✔ A contact number.

✔ A nicer graphic. An invitation to a theme party could include even more stylin' with the artwork.

You and a guest are cordially invited to attend a cocktail party to celebrate

JIMMY JOHNSON'S PROMOTION

Barberian's Steak House
9 Elm Street, Toronto
(at Yonge & Dundas)
July 27th 1997,
7 P.M. 9 P.M.

*Music by Sir Spinner Fine Vinyl
*Complimentary hors d'oeuvres
*Your first two drinks are on the house
*Formal wear, evening gowns, and polyester leisure suits are encouraged

YOUR PRESENCE IS REQUIRED — PRESENTS ARE NOT

To RSVP or for more information, please contact Art Vandelay 1-(800) 555-5555

Figure 5-2: This invitation will lure people to the party.

✔ The entertainment and dress code. These items increase your attendance.

✔ A note about gifts. By telling people they needn't buy gifts, you are also reminding them that they may.

Making a simple invitation

Here's how I might do a simple invitation to a small party.

1. **Establish the theme.**

   I talk about the need to establish your theme in Chapter 1 and give you some great theme ideas in Part II. Your invitation must be consistent with your theme.

2. **On a scrap piece of paper, sketch out a rough idea of what you want to go where on your invitation.**

   In addition to the basic information outlined earlier in this section, leave some room for artwork. I often use photos, but just a drawing or two may suffice.

3. **Search for other ways to make your invitation distinctive.**

   Go to an art supply store and search for self-adhesive letters, borders, and artwork that conveys your theme. If your party is for under 20 people, perhaps you want to personalize each invitation. You may wish to purchase bright colored markers or chalk to hand-color a photocopied card. An art supply store usually has a better price and selection than your local corner store.

   Also consider using a computer to create your invitation. Unless you've just crawled out from under a rock, you or someone you know has access to a computer. Many people would rather do their artwork on a computer. This is okay, but be sure to personalize the invitation somehow. Use an image, not just words. Make it stand out. Computer graphics with a program like Microsoft Publisher give you the most options.

4. **Following your plan, lay the items out on a clean, white sheet of paper.**

   Your invitation should contain color whenever possible. Do you have an eye for color? If not, for goodness sake, get help! Asking for a second or third opinion is not a bad idea.

If you haven't studied art or don't feel you know enough about color, but insist on going it alone, I recommend that you go to a paint store and look at the paint swatches. Often you can find large swatches that assist the novice painter and have several colors that work together. By using a computer you should be able to get close enough to the shades desired.

5. Take the invitation to a print shop or a copying center to print.

Nothing beats the look of a great art layout and a real print job. But printing requires a setup fee and usually starts at $50 for a minimum run. Printing is not really worth the price unless you're printing hundreds of invitations. Photocopying is most cost-effective. I often like to put two invites on a regular-sized sheet of paper and color photocopy them, providing the party is under forty guests. (Twenty color copies is within reason; 100 is usually not.)

Other considerations

The process for making invitations for a large party is virtually the same as making invitations for a small party. However, you are more likely to have three other factors to weigh:

- ✔ **Photos.** If you look closely at photographs in newspapers or magazines, you'll see that they are actually a series of dots. This technique helps prevent the ink from splotching together and produces better reproductions. Care must be taken if you're copying or printing photos; you'll need to make half-tones or they'll end up looking terrible. If you're at a well-stocked copy shop, they'll probably sell sheets of half-tone plastic that you can place over your photo. But if you're really going for a classy look, then take your photo to a photo lab and get a proper half-tone made of it.

  Normally, any decent photocopier has a special button that enhances the quality of a photo. I always recommend going to a professional copy shop and letting them do the work. After all, the personnel are trained to know what works best. Copiers at home or the office are not always as good.

✔ **Paper stock.** Unless your theme dictates otherwise, using high-quality paper is the norm. Try to get the thickest paper you can. I like a white, 70–80 lb card stock because the ink sits on it very nicely and the print also looks raised. However, many photocopy shops won't use thick card stock, which can clog or damage the machine.

✔ **Extra treats.** Maybe you have a small photo, toy, or trinket that you want to include with your invitation. Perhaps you are having a Desert Island theme party and you want to put the message inside a bottle. For a Tiki party, you can include an Easter Island key chain. If you add something, check with the post office for mailing regulations and proper postage.

Other options

Generic invitations are simply an easy way out, but getting something appropriate is not always so easy. If you're lucky, and you find a great package of tasteful cards that work with your theme — congratulations! I've rarely found something that is better than a custom-made card, but sometimes you find appropriate vintage cards at a flea market, garage sale, or novelty store. The problem is, you'll rarely find a complete package of them. In this case, you may want to scan the invite on your computer.

Before you copy an existing invitation, a quick disclaimer concerning copyright laws: The "fun police" aren't going to go after someone who invites a few friends over for dinner with an invitation that uses a picture that has not been cleared for reproduction rights. If you are doing a larger event, however, I highly recommend making sure that you cannot get in trouble for copying without permission. Your local copy shop knows the letter of the law and often posts it for customers.

When I throw really large events (ones that carry a cover charge for admission and don't really fit into the stereotypical "cocktail party" mold), I occasionally use services such as Ticketmaster or Ticketron. These companies charge a service fee above my door charge. The convenient thing of course, is that anyone can call Ticketmaster, order over the phone, and pay with a credit card. Still, only on very rare occasions do I use mass ticket printing. It has no style.

Invitation Etiquette

A few ground rules apply when sending and receiving invitations to cocktail parties. Following cocktail etiquette separates you from many of the others. The host always appreciates the time to reply to an invitation and the guest is more likely to show up if he or she is given adequate notice.

Are you familiar with the postal service and how long it will take via "snail mail," as e-mail fanatics like to call it? You can ask at any post office. Then add a few days to be safe. Sending your invitations two to three weeks before the event is your best bet for in-town guests. Give out-of-town guests four to six weeks. People should have enough time to put the event on their calendar, but not enough time to forget about it.

Double-check all your addresses. People tend to move around a great deal these days; confirming your information can prevent offending a guest who doesn't receive the invitation due to a move. Checking addresses also gives you a chance to let your guests know something is coming in the mail for them or to check the date with them before sending the invitation out.

If you're dealing with a small group of friends, then you can keep it simple. Call them, get their addresses, and if you need to get a zip code, look that up at the post office.

If you're building up a bigger mailing list, the easiest way to do so is on a computer. Whatever the case, once you get over about fifty people, you are going to need a mailing list. But for any type of party with class, you do not want to use normal font computer label printouts. For a large party, you may need to enlist some help in hand-addressing the invitations nicely. Whatever the case, don't let your invitations look like junk mail.

Things to keep in mind when you're sending invitations

Following are a few pointers on the details that get your invitation to your guests. If you heed the advice, the invitation will actually provoke a response.

✔ For the envelope address, always write in ink — as nicely as possible — or use a unique computer font that doesn't look like junk mail. You are going for the personal look.

✔ For a formal invitation, use no abbreviations. Spell everything out, with the exception of state or province names. (Most post offices prefer that you use abbreviations for those.)

✔ Never put "and family" on the invitation. Send individual invitations.

I can hardly even imagine anyone asking if children are allowed at cocktail parties, but the only proper answer would be "What part of 'No' don't you understand?" A cocktail party is most decidedly not a children's event. Everybody loves children, but the whole idea of the cocktail party is mingling and drinking with a certain amount of sophistication — children and booze don't mix.

✔ Never send bulk mail or have your invitations meter-canceled. Use stamps, and pick out a stamp that fits the mood of your party, if possible.

✔ Everything you do should have your own personal touch. If you really want to put the touch of class on an invitation, then go buy some sealing wax (it comes in various colors) and a metal stamp.

Where am I going to put them all?

When I started putting on parties, I'd invite a hundred people and twenty people would show up. Then I invited thirty people and two hundred people showed up. Now, I tend to make the invitation so clear that my attendance projections are more accurate. No matter how strictly you follow this book, there is always a chance that the number of people expected don't show. Don't be frustrated by any early lack of attendance at your parties. If you love the idea of being a party host, then start small and just keep putting on great parties. People will show up.

Things to keep in mind when responding to an invitation

RSVP stands for *Repondez s'il vous plait,* meaning "Respond, please." The cocktail party tradition is to RSVP. The purpose is so that the host knows how many people to expect for the catering requirements. A modern twist on this response is RSVP by answering machine, fax, and e-mail. Normally, the invitation specifies how you should respond. Responding to someone's business fax machine is tacky if she has asked you to leave a message on her home phone.

If you are a guest and are asked to RSVP, then it is your cocktail etiquette duty to respond, whether or not you are attending. Many people think that they should only respond if they plan on attending, but the host greatly appreciates hearing back from you either way. At least he knows that the invitation arrived, and if someone asks why you aren't there, your host has a story to tell.

Many people choose to go with another method that asks people to only respond if they're not attending. Do so like this: "Regrets Only. 555-4321." This message is not as specific, and you run the risk of expecting many more people than you may get.

The RSVP is really all about the outlay of money. You want to know how much food and liquor to buy. A guest shoulders the responsibility of responding in a timely fashion, and if he has responded "yes" then it's his responsibility to show up. If an emergency comes up and he can't attend, he should call, e-mail, or fax his regrets.

When a guest is invited to a cocktail party, cocktail etiquette assumes that he will bring a date if he wants. If you're asked to RSVP, however, then respond with "Myself" or "My date and I will definitely be attending." That way, the host can plan accordingly. It's expected that a guest will bring a spouse or regular date. If, on the other hand, you decide you want to bring along a friend or business associate, cocktail etiquette dictates that you check with the host first.

You make the choice of whether or not you expect people to RSVP. If you want them to, you need to clearly state so on the invitation. You'll want your RSVP to be a phone message number, a fax, and/or an e-mail address. People turning down the invitation don't want to talk to you, they just want to leave the obligatory polite regret. And you don't really want to talk to them, either, because they're missing the party of the century.

How many of the invited guests will show up? That's hard to determine. Unfortunately, in spite of all you do, some people will not respond, and some people will respond and then never show up. People have become so busy, so lax, and so overwhelmed by junk mail that they will sometimes ignore an RSVP.

Don't count on using your RSVPs to determine how many people will be attending your party. They will give you a ballpark figure at least, but they're rarely, if ever, totally accurate. Always allow for give and take when it comes to numbers at your bash.

All formal invitations should be accepted with pleasure or refused with regret. If responses are written, they should be handwritten in the same literary style and layout as the original invitation.

Do something nice for your host

Sometimes my guests send me a nice postcard to let me know that they can't make it. It's a great keepsake, and I'll often pass it around the party before toasting the preoccupied person. Sending a card is a great deal of trouble to go through, and I don't take it for granted!

Chapter 6

Ambiance — Creating the Right Mood

● ●

In This Chapter

▶ Art director

▶ Colors

▶ Lighting

▶ Decorating

● ●

A great and memorable party has four essential ingredients:

✔ A great group of guests

✔ Good atmosphere

✔ Good music and entertainment

✔ Good food and drink consistent with the theme

This chapter focuses on the atmosphere, or the ambiance. Through your decorations, your lighting, and your use of space, you want to reinforce your theme and put people into party mode the minute that they walk into your room. Doing so takes a little imagination, some planning, and some work, but is well worth the effort.

Decor: The First Impression

If you are fortunate enough to live in a space-age bachelor pad, own a mansion, or have a friend with an awesome space for a party, you are indeed fortunate. You know that your guests will be wowed when they walk through the door. Those who don't, however, have to worry about making a good first impression.

The lighting, colors, and appearance of your door staff tell your guests that they're in for a treat the minute they get to the door. The right first impression can cause a skeptic to stare in awe. I've seen it happen, and knowing that someone can be convinced that he's in for a great time within moments of arriving is a great ego boost for the host.

You will be expected to restore your party venue to its pre-party state of existence. Make your decorating as easy or complicated as you want, but don't forget that you need to clean up afterward and that you must not destroy the venue's hardwood walls or painted surfaces.

Color

People pick up most of their information visually, and your color scheme tells your guests a great deal about your party. Remember, after you decide what the mood and theme is, you want to try to make sure that everything you do reinforces that theme. Is the party going to be formal? Black-and-white in tone? Or are you going to interject a color scheme? Whatever you decide, stay consistent with everything from napkins to table coverings.

One color at a time

The greatest color theme party I ever attended was at a place called the "Funny Farm" in a small, rural community in Southwestern Ontario, Canada. Every room in the large farmhouse was painted a different color, and every item in the room matched. Can you imagine walking into a turquoise room and finding everything from the sofa and carpet to the ashtray and telephone to be the exact same color? So much effort went into this installation that it was obviously meant to be permanent. There were rooms in pink, green, beige, and white.

Our hosts, Laura and Gordon, had a walk-in closet filled with appropriate clothes in matching colors for the various rooms. The outfits varied in size, and everybody found something she liked. They hired a photographer to take Polaroids of the guests in each room. Naturally, after ten minutes or so, the guests were encouraged to go from room to room and mingle with the other colors.

My favorite example of a multicolored theme party is the Rubik's Cube Party that you can read about in Chapter 4.

Your color scheme doesn't even have to be complicated. A party of all one color can be very effective. An all-red room, with all-red food and drinks, can really set a mood. Or all-blue. You can pick food and drinks that are already one color. Where nature doesn't provide, use food coloring.

Basic decorating materials

Decorating possibilities and solutions are limited only by your budget and your imagination, and often someone with a good imagination can save a great deal of money by using cheaper materials like cardboard and crepe paper. Always try to make, borrow, or rent — in that preferred order — any items you need.

To plan or not to plan: That is the decorating question

A cocktail party is all about class and consistency; it should not look like a hodge-podge of ideas thrown together. If you feel comfortable taking on the task of planning all of the decorations for your party, then go for it. If you don't, then appoint or hire a designated art director.

The art director is the person who is responsible for that classy, consistent look, from the invitations to the decorations to the selection of food and music. How do you find an art director? You have two choices. Think of a friend who dresses great and has a great-looking apartment; that's a good sign that she knows how to decorate. Otherwise, hire one. You can find an art director by asking around at clubs, theaters, or film companies.

A good art director can be someone who creates window displays, is a fashion stylist, or works in props or set design in theater, film, or music videos. When you see a good-looking restaurant or club, ask who designed the rooms. After you find the person, you will immediately want to discuss the date, size, and budget of your cocktail party to the level of art director's involvement or interest.

(continued)

(continued)

Don't feel bad if you're not naturally inclined toward art direction; just have the common sense to delegate. People love the job. It's really fun, and it's a big ego booster at the party when those in attendance compliment the person who did the design. Just remember that if you are confident enough in someone's abilities to delegate responsibility to her, then you absolutely must let her make some of the decisions. Don't just give somebody a nice title and not let her do anything. Put her to work!

The "must have" decorating supply list

Many a host has arrived at a venue or a friend's home only to find that some essential tools aren't available. As you make plans to decorate make a checklist of the things you'll need to get the job done.

✔ **Duct tape:** The gray, sticky, theater type. If you're trying to hide the tape, you can buy it in black. A theater supply house or a major hardware store carries different colors. You can never have enough of this stuff, so stock up. Don't expect the venue to provide duct tape, because people have a tendency to walk away with the stuff.

✔ **A hand-held staple gun:** Get a small one. The larger ones are hand-fatiguing and unnecessary. Buy $5/16$-inch staples.

✔ **Some heavy fish line:** This tool can really come in handy if you're trying to hang things from the ceiling in a nice-looking way. In a darkened room, fishing line can give the impression that an object is levitating on its own.

✔ **Butcher paper, cardboard, and packing tubes.** Remember how high school clubs always used butcher paper and poster paint for assemblies and announcements? They did so because the material was cheap and effective. If you have butcher paper and poster paint and a friend who knows how to paint, then he can work wonders in a short amount of time. He can do the painting elsewhere — outside if possible — let the works dry, and roll them up for the party. Styrofoam is readily available and can work wonders, too.

✔ **Extension cords:** You can never have too many power cords. Get both short ones and long ones. You may also require a power bar. Don't expect the venue to supply them, as people are always walking out with them.

✔ **Scissors or a good knife.**

✔ **A flashlight:** Most clubs and venues are dark and inadequately lit. I've often thought that people who work in clubs should be issued a miner's flashlight on their heads. Dark rooms look great when everyone's drinking and chattering and having fun, but they're often hard to work in when you're setting up. Bring a flashlight.

✔ **Milk crates or similar containers:** These work great for carrying your tape, power cords, and staple guns. They also stack nicely in the back of a vehicle. The added bonus is that they work well as table a when you need something to set a light or a projector on. Some simple fabric can be used to cover them and hide what they really are.

Other decorating items you may need

Go through your decorating requirements and assess which, if any, of these you'll need.

Ladders	Posterboard
X-acto blade knives	Construction paper
	Tissue paper
A screwdriver	Rubber cement
Paint, paint brushes, and cleanup rags	Masking tape
A hammer and a few nails	Spray paint
	Cardboard
Pliers	String
A bucket	Balloons
A small saw	Finishing nails
Straight pins	Small eyelet screws
Push pins	Thumbtacks
Crepe paper	

Basic decorating ideas

I've said it before, and I'll say it again. Everything about your party — especially your decorations — should be tied to your cocktail party theme. Chapters 3 and 4 have a number of decorating ideas for particular party themes, but no single book can have a conclusive list. Besides, you want to use your own imagination and personality.

What follows is a sampling of ideas for particular decorating challenges. Even if you don't find exactly what you need, you will get an idea or two and some tips to help you create your perfect cocktail setting.

Stay with the big picture. Concern yourself with the large things that will make the most impact. Don't worry about small and time-consuming detail decorations until everything else is finished.

Hanging items

Hanging items are great to create a mood, hide an ugly ceiling, or create a more intimate atmosphere in a room with a too-high ceiling.

If you're doing a go-go early '60s theme, you can hang kitsch items above the heads of the gathered guests. You don't have to spend a great deal of money — the decorations can be shapes cut out of card stock, women's shoes, or almost anything. This type of decoration can be very effective, but also very time-consuming. You'll need fishing line, a staple gun, a ladder, someone to spot the ladder, and plenty of time to do it.

I was at a party where the hosts made a "chandelier" out of plastic baggies. The baggies were filled with water and hung. Each one had a live goldfish inside. It was very effective.

Most venues that run live entertainment already have hooks, wires, and nails on the walls and ceilings that have been left behind by others. Try to use those first.

If you have a venue with a high ceiling and you're trying to create a more intimate effect, then try criss-crossing invisible wire at the desired level by using screw eyes or even just tape. Hang decorations from this wire and create a false-ceiling effect. *Note:* You're going to need to consider fire hazards. Flame-retardant materials and paint are available from theater supply houses and fire safety supply houses.

When you're putting up anything, make sure that you get permission from the venue manager to put tacks in the ceilings or to use a staple gun. Forget masking tape — for a party, it's all held together with duct tape or staples. But do be careful, because tape can pull paint right off the wall. Also, remember to make things look nice; take the time to hide your tape and your electrical cables.

Walls

If you find yourself in a large room with blank walls, don't despair! You have many options for decorating the walls that will enhance the ambiance of your cocktail party. Here are just a few ideas:

- ✔ **Hang objects on the wall.** A few palm fronds do wonders for a South Pacific theme, for example. Maybe you're in a white room and you want a flowery look. Sometimes you can pin fabric to the ceiling or even tape it onto the wall. You need to look at the situation, be aware of fire safety, and work toward making the ambiance of a room match your theme.

- ✔ **Project images onto the wall.** An easy way to make your room to look as cool as your favorite art gallery or dance club is with slides or movies. The great thing about using slides or movies is that you're not hanging or stapling things up on walls. The only problem is that you need to find an area that you can place the projector. And light has to have something to project onto, so if you're in a black or brick-walled room, you may have to create white surfaces to catch the lights or projections (see next bulleted item for ideas).

What should you show? For a slide show, have some slides made that are consistent with your theme. You can have a friend take slides of groovy old album covers if you're having a retro party, or perhaps a beautiful sculpture garden in a nearby park for an elegant soiree. A simple and humorous slide show also can be very effective, but don't make guests sit and watch slides from your summer vacation.

Eight- or 16-millimeter film projectors also can create a great effect. A movie — pertaining to your theme — can be run on a wall without sound in its entirety. Or you can show dance routines from musicals (*That's Entertainment, Part III* has lots of dance routines). Or you can do what the dance halls do and run a short tape loop. A loop is not hard to do and can add a great ambiance to your party. If you don't feel comfortable technically, find a technically-minded friend and have her help you out.

If you're on a budget, many libraries and college media centers will let you check slide or movie projectors out for a couple of days. Thrift stores such as Goodwill and Salvation Army often have outdated slide projectors that — with a new bulb — can work fine for your needs.

When you use projectors, you're going to have to run AC extension cords for those projectors. Be careful to place the cords out of harm's way. The house technician at a venue or a technically-minded person at home comes in very handy here.

✔ **Project images on something in front of the walls.** Remember the kid in grade school who always stuck his hands up in front of the movie projector when the teacher wasn't looking? Well, that same basic effect can work very well at your party. For example, import shops sell Japanese white paper balls that can be wonderful to project onto at any size party. The paper balls come in different sizes and are opened up and hung.

For larger venues, you can try more dramatic solutions without spending a lot. For example, if you have enough space, hang up a whole sheet of white fabric or muslin. Behind the muslin, hang objects from the ceiling: Tiki gods work nicely, for example, for a Tiki theme. You then set up backlights behind them, casting their shadows onto the fabric. Don't worry about the fabric hanging straight or tight; the movement and flutter makes the effect look more interesting. To the crowd drinking and mingling, you have a wall of interesting-looking figures that goes with your theme.

Be very careful about fire dangers when hanging fabric of any kind for a party. The fabric or curtains used in clubs are normally flame-proofed. To be safe, go to a theater supply house and buy fabric that is already flame-proofed.

Slides also don't have to be limited to a wall or fabric. I've seen slides projected onto the sidewalk right outside of a party. I've seen slides projected onto fabric hanging from a tree in the backyard. I've seen slides and even movies projected onto the wall of a building right across the street. The possibilities are endless.

I saw this effect in a backyard tent once. You couldn't go into the tent; it was just a great visual. It was simple; all kinds of shadows on the outside tent walls were being created by a light source inside the tent shining onto a paper mobile.

✔ **Use light to disguise the wall.** If you don't have an audio-visual budget, put a colored floodlight inside a plastic milk crate and point the light up at the wall. This creates a large, soft beam of light with a grated pattern. Just put the light in a location that won't pose a danger to your guests or staff.

Floors

A little confetti goes a long way. If you notice stains on the carpet or an unattractive floor, toss a few bags of paper confetti around. Confetti looks festive and is fairly easy to vacuum.

Try to avoid plastic confetti. Keep in mind that although the tiny sparkles in plastic confetti may look good, they are very difficult to remove later, so paper confetti is usually preferred.

Unusual situations

If you plan on doing major decorating in a venue, then take a few tips from the pros.

✔ If your room contains large obstacles like pillars, basketball hoops, and storage lockers, then integrate them into your visual concept. Turn obstacles into new shapes to play with. Cover them with painted butcher paper, thread vines around them, or stick artificial fruit on them.

✔ If you don't have the time or money to completely decorate the entire party space, then do what the big designers do. Pick the focal point, go all out there, and gradually taper down to less as you move away from that point. Lighting (discussed in detail a little later in this chapter) helps immensely to accentuate certain areas and hide less visually pleasing places.

✔ If you have a swimming pool, make sure that your bar and food are far away from the pool. You do not want to encourage people to dive in after eating and drinking. If you plan on using the pool, appoint a token lifeguard. You'll obviously want to make sure that the pool has been cleaned recently, but also look into borrowing or renting extra deck chairs and small tables. Perhaps you can find lamps, candles, or small statues that add to the theme of your party.

Lights, Lights, Action

The perfect amount of lighting is more important than the type. No matter how small your budget, you can make that room filled with fluorescent lights much dimmer or turn the dark basement into a brighter, more pleasant place to party. Unattractive lighting will almost certainly cut your party short. Romantic lighting needn't make you sleepy, however; it should enable you to see the whole room but not encourage the use of sunglasses at night!

Kinds of lighting

You'll rarely use just the existing room light for a cocktail party. Such light is usually just too harsh to put people into the party mood. Here are some alternatives to consider:

✔ **String lights and party lights.** Christmas lights can sometimes set the right mood, even if it's not Christmas. A long string of tiny blue lights for a Blue Hawaii theme can work well, or a long string of tiny white lights on a ceiling can be stars.

Many party or kitsch-type stores sell other types of string lights. You can find Japanese lanterns, carnival lights, Tiki lights, tropical fish, fruit, and red pepper lights. Not to mention baseballs, footballs, basketballs, American flags, dinosaurs, sunflowers, bees, desert skulls and boots, and pink flamingos.

After you determine your theme, decide if any of these items will be appropriate. Remember that a party store is a good place to get ideas, but try to come up with your own art vision rather than just buying stuff.

✔ **Patio lanterns.** From lasers to patio lanterns, this is quite a section! Patio lanterns are fun and rarely too bright. However, they usually are very cheaply made, so

Make your bathroom fit the theme when you have a house party

 Contrary to what some single men may think, your party decorating obligations do not end at the bathroom door. In fact, no matter how much effort you put into decorations, if your bathroom is a mess, that's what some guests will remember!

Do you have to work as hard decorating the bathroom as other rooms? Of course not. Just keep two things in mind:

- **Cleanliness.** Men, this may come as a shock, but women will not tolerate an unclean bathroom. Keep the place clean for the female guests who are all dressed up.

- **Ambiance.** Again, don't go overboard. At least have air freshener. If you're having a large party and several people will be moving through, you want a candle burning and some kind of potpourri or something that smells good, but is *not* a generic, hospital-smelling clean. You want something that has a pleasant odor. Coconut-scented air fresheners smell great and — because of their Polynesian flavor — are quite popular now for cocktail party bathrooms.

If the sexes will have separate bathrooms, pay careful attention to the women's bathroom. Make sure that the bathroom has special scented soap and flowers in addition to potpourri. Consider putting some reading materials in the men's restroom — sports, comics, or news. Something with pictures   kitsch, light, and fun. You don't want someone spending hours reading in there. If possible, make the reading material correspond to the party theme.

Based on my experience, some people will go through your bathroom cabinets just to see what's in there. Party-proof your bathroom; put stuff in there that you don't care if people see and get rid of stuff that you don't want people to see. If you have anything private, you don't want it in the public bathroom.

be sure to check the lanterns immediately after purchase! The lanterns can be used for various theme parties or a traditional cocktail soiree. Only the most elegant events can afford to snub a patio lantern.

✔ **Strobe lights.** These flashing lights are not for cocktail parties. Discos can keep them. Being in a room lit only with strobes is unhealthy, especially when drinking; guests are more likely to have accidents because of the uneven lighting. Strobes are for fun houses in amusement parks, not in your house to amuse your guests.

✔ **Lasers.** If you think I'm going to knock using these at cocktail parties, I'm going to fool you. Using lasers to create intrigue or make guests relax is much better than the strobe-flashing freakout of a full-blown disco. One of the best uses I've ever seen was at a party for the film *Whale Music.* As guests entered up a long, dark hall, lasers created a beautiful, calm wave to the sounds of whales singing.

Unless you're doing a huge event, you likely don't have the space or the budget for lasers, but if you do, there are no shortcuts. You must hire a specialist to work them.

After you pick out your lights, you have to decide how you want to use them. In addition to direct lighting — just shining the lights straight at your guests — consider these two techniques:

✔ **Spotlighting.** This consists of highlighting and focusing lights on the primary area of the room — the part of the room that is the most visually pleasing.

✔ **Indirect lighting.** This consists of creating an aura of lower light in areas where you want to have a mood going, but you don't want the light to be too bright. Focus the lights onto the ceiling, or turn some of the lights off, or go with lower wattage in order to achieve the desired effect.

Smoke and mirrors — and bubble machines?

Closely related to the topic of lights are three items occasionally seen at parties — mirror balls, bubble machines, and smoke machines.

A mirror ball is always a bonus at a cocktail party, but not always worth renting. If you use one, you have to make sure that someone understands where to project the light so the room is covered. Normally you want two small pin lights (lights with tightly focused beams) in opposite corners of a room.

The problem with mirror balls is that most people don't know when to turn them off. A mirror ball should really only be used to heighten certain moments — maybe your favorite Tony Bennett song for a slow dance — and not used for hours on end. It can make people dizzy after a spell.

Bubble machines can be dangerous. These machines are normally part of a performance, either on a stage or dance floor, but no matter where you aim it, liquid is left on the floor somewhere. This liquid is dangerous for dancers and can damage musical equipment. A good place to use a bubble machine is over the front door of your house or cottage. As long as you make sure that you lay plenty of carpet so no one slips on the way in, your guests will get a kick out of seeing your house bubbling as they enter.

Smoke machines should not be used at a cocktail party unless the space is huge, and then only if the machine is used for stage purposes. I say this from first-hand experience. I was involved with a terrific party for Wes Craven (director of *Nightmare on Elm Street*) where fog was required. The folks at Alliance Pictures had rented out The Arts and Letters Club on Elm Street to throw a party for the premiere of his movie at the Toronto International Film Festival. Bodies hung from the ceiling of this old wooden building. The stage looked more like an altar, with countertenor Carl Strygg, jazz diva Holly Cole, and sitarist/bassist George Koller performing in a floor of fog. The problem wasn't the fog from the stage, though. Someone had rigged a machine to pour down the stairs from the balcony. This caused more than one person to wipe out, spilling a drink and feeling embarrassed. Other than the poor planning of the second smoke machine, the party was flawless.

Lighting at a house party — creating a mood

Great lighting can almost save a bad room. If you're having a house party, you likely won't need a lighting designer, but you will need to look at your lighting at the same time of day that your party is going to take place and ask yourself how the room is going to look filled with people. If you're going for a party during the quintessential cocktail party hour — and the room has windows — then you want to try and work in the feeling of the sun going down.

Take a close look at the lamps that are in your party room. Turn the lights on at the same time of day that your party's going to take place. How does the room look? How does the room feel? Is it too bright? The lighting should be gentle on the eyes. You want a flattering level of light in which people can look and feel beautiful.

If the lighting is too bright, you need to deal with it. If your kitchen has four-foot fluorescent lights overhead, you're going to have a few options:

- ✔ Turn the lights off and don't use them.

- ✔ Go to a lighting supply house and buy colored gel sheaths to slip over the fluorescent lights. *Gels* are thin transparent or translucent pieces of colored plastic that are used in stage, photography, and film. They are an inexpensive way to "color up" a room and, in the case of a cocktail party, keep the room nice and dim. A pink gel is available that will tone down fluorescent lights.

- ✔ Become familiar with theater lighting gel — available at any theater supply house — and pick up a swatch pack. Gel can be taped right over the plastic that covers white fluorescent lights. Or you can use the gels to change the color of lampshades.

Lighting in a venue — creating a mood for a bigger party

You've decided what your theme is. Perhaps you consulted a Hawaiian travel brochure or watched a movie to prepare you for an Elegant and Sophisticated Soiree. You've had this image in your mind — now try to recall the warm lighting. You want to duplicate the feeling you get from watching or reading about the perfect party — and with a little forethought into that magical amount of lighting required, you can! A "trip light" such as a lava light, glitter lamp, spinning light, and so on can be a terrific bonus, but it's the overall level you have to worry about. Beautiful old lamps are incredibly inexpensive at thrift stores and yard sales. If your lights don't have dimmers, a 40-watt bulb works best in most lamps.

Of course, in larger rooms you will ideally speak with a house technician, and perhaps your plans can be a little more elaborate.

With your party needs in mind, do a walk-through of the room. Look for AC outlets and think about where things are and what else you may need. Make a list. For safety purposes, be aware of where fire extinguishers and breaker panels are located.

Blown breakers = Potentially blown party

WARNING! If you're bringing in your own lighting to a venue, or adding a great deal of lighting to the venue's existing electrical outlets, then you run the danger of blowing breakers and creating a fire hazard. The reason: The large lighting systems that rock bands and dance clubs use do not run off of the normal household electrical current that you're used to. You don't need to learn all about it, but you do need to know that you can't just start plugging things in anywhere you see an open outlet.

Consult with someone who knows — preferably the technician at the club. He may also be able to plug your lights into his dimmer pack, a safe option that also gives you control over the intensity of the lights. You just have to be careful about fire concerns and taping down cables so guests don't trip over them.

Lighting in rented rooms

The venue that you're renting will have one of three different lighting situations going on:

✔ Basic lighting in the room. The bar and mingle area are probably on a simple dimmer switch.

✔ Same as above but with four to six little spotlights, also on a dimmer, for the entertainment stage. You may be able to refocus these lights.

✔ Big production, sound, and lights, usually being rented from an independent production company. These kinds of situations have a production person that runs the system, and he doesn't want you messing around with it unless he's there. You may get these lights thrown in with your room rental deal or you may have to negotiate for them separately.

Many venues already have decent lighting, particularly if they run live entertainment. What you need to do is get together with the house production person and have her show you what's available and what you can do with it. In general, house production people show up during the late afternoon or early evening and hang out for the rest of the night. Catch them at a time when they're not busy and slip them a few bucks if you take up a lot of their time.

If a venue has extensive overhead lighting for disco or live entertainment, the lights most definitely can be refocused onto walls and such to help set the mood. A production person for the venue is going to have to refocus the lights for you. After your party, he's going to need to refocus it all back. Depending on how extensive that lighting is, focusing may take an hour or more each time. If your needs are demanding, you should pay the lighting technician a little extra for his help. If the venue is already paying him to be there, slipping him as little as $20 makes the job easier.

When you first go through the room with the booking agent or manager, make sure that you know whether extra costs are involved for technical help or lighting. Negotiate immediately.

If you're working in a rented venue, your best bet is to utilize the qualified people that are already working there. Talk to the lighting designer or technical person about your needs and the mood that you're trying to create. This person needs to know three things:

> ✔ What is the color scheme or mood of the party?
>
> ✔ Where are the areas that need to be well lit? Hors d'oeuvres? Entertainment?
>
> ✔ Where are the areas that need to be more subtly lit for mingling?

The venue production people are already going to know where the ladders are. They are going to have some kind of supply of colored light gels, but you'll want to talk about their supply in advance because you may want to go and purchase some new ones.

Whatever the case, in general the people working in clubs are a bit underpaid, but will be of great assistance to you. When you make your rental agreement, you should determine if you're getting lighting and a production person.

The Space and Layout of the Party

Whether you are throwing the party at home or at a venue, think about the type of party you are throwing, and ask if the layout — how the furniture is arranged in the rooms — supports or detracts from your plans. And then ask yourself three critical questions:

1. **Does my furniture encourage guests to mingle, or does it get in the way?**

2. **Are the bar and the hors d'oeuvres table conveniently located, or are they obtrusive?**

3. **If you're having a dance floor and/or band, is the furniture in the logical spot for the guests?**

To illustrate the first point, look at Figure 6-1. The couch on the left is a typical living room arrangement — but all wrong for a cocktail party.

Why? Because the guests on the couch have their backs to other guests! A traditional one- or two-room cocktail party is all about standing, mingling, and chattering. Your job — in the grand tradition of the cocktail party — is to maximize "chance encounters" by creating movement and paths in order for your guests to both approach and escape each other. The guests on the couch can go the entire party without making eye contact with guests at the rear of the room if the conversation keeps them interested.

Here's another truism that illustrates point 2: Guests will find the bar. For that reason, the bar on the left in Figure 6-2 is incorrectly placed.

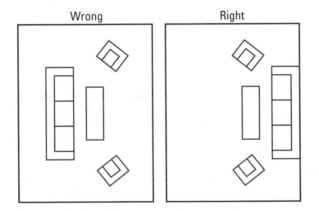

Figures 6-1: A couch in the middle of the room, left, is an unwelcome obstacle to mingling at your cocktail party.

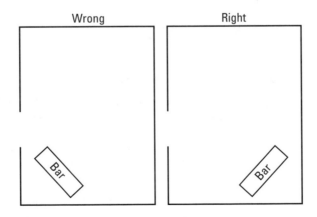

Figures 6-2: A bar too close to the entrance discourages the guest from exploring the room.

You want your guests to see your room while heading to the bar. Motivate them to get out of the corner, to explore a little, as shown in the right side of Figure 6-2. Also, guests tend to congregate around the bar, so placing the bar as in the left side of Figure 6-2 clogs up the entrance.

Bar placement is, of course, sometimes limited by where you have a sink. I've often been to parties where the host simply blocked off the kitchen with a table, a table that he then used for the bar. It was simple but effective, and saved the cost of renting a bar!

In addition to putting your bar away from the entrance, make sure that your other furniture doesn't limit access to the bar. Although having a few chairs near the bar is a good idea at larger venues because it gives people who meet in line a convenient place to go and talk, make sure that you have enough room for the people still waiting in line.

Food placement — if you're not using a waiting staff — is somewhat tied to bar placement. You want the hors d'oeuvres table to be somewhat close to the bar, but not next to the bar. You also don't want the crowd at the hors d'oeuvres table clogging the entrance. An incorrect food placement is shown on the left in Figure 6-3, while a good food placement is shown on the right.

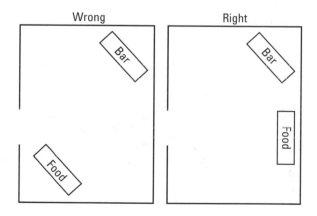

Figures 6-3: Food should be somewhat close to the bar and away from the entrance.

Finally, keep in mind that

- ✔ Guests will sit where there are tables
- ✔ Guests will stand and mingle in open areas
- ✔ Guests who are standing are more likely to join in dancing

For these reasons, you don't want to separate your open areas and your dance floor with a block of tables, as shown on the left in Figure 6-4. Instead, you want something where the mingling area blends into the dance floor.

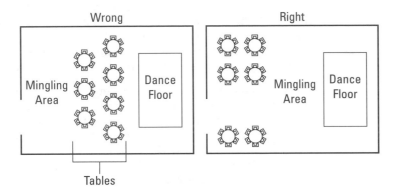

Figures 6-4: Don't discourage standing guests from dancing by putting a wall of tables between them and the dance floor.

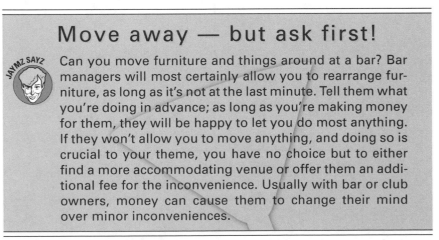

Move away — but ask first!

JAYMZ SAYZ Can you move furniture and things around at a bar? Bar managers will most certainly allow you to rearrange furniture, as long as it's not at the last minute. Tell them what you're doing in advance; as long as you're making money for them, they will be happy to let you do most anything. If they won't allow you to move anything, and doing so is crucial to your theme, you have no choice but to either find a more accommodating venue or offer them an additional fee for the inconvenience. Usually with bar or club owners, money can cause them to change their mind over minor inconveniences.

Remember to put a couple of chairs near the edge of the dance floor, in case someone needs to sit down for a minute after a tantalizing tango!

A couple of other points to remember about layout in a single room:

✔ Put your band (if you have one) in the farthest corner possible. Having people walking in front is distracting to band members and makes them feel less important. By this placement, you also minimize foot traffic in areas where you'll probably have power cables.

✔ Don't put anything near the kitchen door that encourages guests to congregate there! You don't want a fully loaded waiter and a guest to have a collision. A polite warning sign sometimes helps.

✔ Do put tables near the restrooms so that guests have a place to put their drinks before they go inside. Otherwise, don't impede restroom traffic.

✔ If you are allowing smoking, then you need to have several ashtrays out. If you don't own ashtrays, they can be rented from a party supply house.

✔ If you're throwing a house party, leave out some end tables for those ashtrays and empty drink glasses.

Figure 6-5 shows a good layout for a large single room. The bar and the band are away from the entrance; the furniture encourages eye contact and mingling, without walling off the dance floor; and the kitchen entrance is clear.

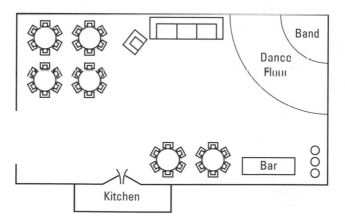

Figure 6-5: A nicely arranged cocktail party room.

For a longer party or a multi-room party, have one "stand up and mingle" room. But you also want — if your space allows — to create other rooms for other moods. In order to make everyone mingle and chatter for the first hour or so, think about keeping those rooms closed off for awhile. As the party continues into the evening, you can open up other areas for dancing and more intimate mingling. The host or the door person is responsible for making sure that everyone knows the other rooms are available and open.

Some guests may get overwhelmed by a large group of people and prefer a small side room or area. Business executives and entertainers are often cornered at parties by someone who wants to schmooze a job out of them or heap praise in embarrassing amounts. Having an intimate room gives these people some place a little dimmer where they can speak with a few people for a while uninterrupted.

If you're throwing a multi-room event, putting bowls of something edible in each room is common. But you only need one bar.

Other furniture no-no's

✔ What you decide to use should be comfortable but shouldn't swallow your guests whole! Huge puffy couches and chairs not only give your guests bad posture, but you run the risk of them falling asleep before very long!

✔ Don't use priceless antiques unless you can afford to fix them. One of your guests may accidentally spill red wine or burn a small hole in the carpet from careless smoking.

While you may want to get a large piece of fabric to cover your sofa, I cannot condone leaving the plastic on your new couch — unless of course you are doing a theme party such as a Square '50s Party, Americana Backyard Barbecue, or TV Night.

✔ If you can't get the exact furniture you want, keep in mind that "less is more," and you'll be okay.

Chapter 7

The Cocktail Party Music Guide

In This Chapter

▶ The who's who in cocktail music

▶ DJs are better than premixed tapes!

▶ Live entertainment or irritainment

*C*ocktails and music, if properly blended, fit together like an olive on a toothpick. If done well, the music at your quintessential cocktail party will conjure up memories of elegant couples in formal attire, waltzing across a glistening hardwood floor under a shimmering chandelier. If you have the right music at your Tiki party, you'll create thoughts of skinny dipping in a warm blue ocean and sunning on a white sand beach. Whatever the theme of your party, the music and entertainment you choose will either enhance or destroy all your hard work.

When you throw a party, you have three basic options for providing music:

✔ Play recorded music yourself.

✔ Ask or hire someone else (a friend or a DJ) to play the music.

✔ Hire a musician or live band.

Each scenario has advantages and disadvantages. Regardless of which option you select, the music has to be consistent with your theme. You don't want to be playing tropical island exotica music at a "South of the Border" party. True, they're both south, but you want to be correct. After the lights go down, you want your sounds and your drinks to blend with each other as one.

This chapter gives you a basic overview of the cocktail music movement and its origins so that you can blend your music and your party, and discusses some of the issues involved in how you provide that music. Remember, all the work you go through ensuring that the ambiance, beverages, and food are perfect won't mean anything if you play inappropriate or obnoxiously loud music at your event.

The Basic Forms of Cocktail Music

When I say cocktail music (some call it *lounge*), I'm talking about a wide range of musicians and styles: big band swing, exotica, Latin, space age pop, and sometimes even instrumental surf. The main characteristic that differentiates cocktail music from other forms of pop music is that while the music is generally danceable, you should be able to hold down a pleasant conversation while the music is playing. If the sound features the buzz and drone of electric guitars and a screaming singer, then it is not cocktail music, and should be avoided at all costs.

Some have disdainfully called cocktail music "Easy Listening Music." Well, as one lounge aficionado said, "How hard should listening to music have to be?" After a long day in this loud modern world, cocktail music can be an odd and unexpectedly refreshing escape from the bombast of both current and classic rock.

Much of this music was never actually all that popular in its time, at least not with young people, but after brewing in the underground for over a decade, lounge and cocktail music have burst out into the mainstream — maybe due to the human craving for intimacy and more communal entertainment. Nearly every major city has venues that support the lounge lifestyle. Plenty of music is available in either re-release or new release, and most every record store now features a large "lounge" or "cocktail" section.

Following is the cocktail party music guide — a comprehensive guide to the various genres of cocktail music. I give you a brief description, talk about a few of the pioneers, and give examples of a few quintessential recordings from the genre. I avoid mentioning records that are not currently available in stores. Some of the best records by Enoch Light, Dick Hyman, and Hugo Montenegro can only be found on vinyl in second hand shops or at yard sales, and therefore have not been included. A lengthy list of available cocktail party music CDs can be found in the appendix.

Compilations

Dozens of record companies are currently pillaging their archives for great cocktail music. The "Ultra-Lounge" series on Capitol/EMI is leading the pack, with over a dozen compilation records. These records are theme-based, making it easy to decide which to purchase for your event. Every song is by a different artist, which adds excitement and variety to your party. Compilations are the next best thing to a DJ.

Examples of the genre:

Cha Cha D'Amour — Ultra Lounge Series (Capitol/EMI)

Swingin Singles — Cocktail Mix Series (Rhino)

Mallets In Wonderland — Space Age Pop Series (BMG)

Space age bachelor pad music

"Space age bachelor pad music" was coined by artist Byron Werner of Los Angeles in the mid-80s to describe a genre of Eisenhower-Kennedy era instrumental pop. Werner said the music was typified by "discordant harmonies, exaggerated stereo effects, zippy, optimistic melodies." The original market, he claimed, was "lonely guys with too much disposable income who are nit-picky about their stereos."

Also called "Space Age Pop," this form of cocktail music was pioneered by Juan Garcia Esquivel, a sound genius who produced some of the most innovative stereo recordings of the '50s and '60s. He expanded the standard palette of orchestra and chorus by using unique and unusual instruments such as the harpsichord, exotic percussion, whistling, humming, and bongos, among other things.

Although a megastar in his native Mexico, Esquivel's original albums were often overlooked in his heyday by the Top 40 mainstream, and they didn't chart in the United States. But his Spike Jones-meets-Dali arrangements and Wagnerian magnificence made lasting impressions and influenced many other artists, myself included.

In his thirty-plus year career, Esquivel has recorded lots of music — mostly released on RCA — and written theme and background music for television series, including *Charlie's Angels, Kojak,* and *Magnum, P.I.* Both BMG and Bar/None records have put out re-issues of his music.

Examples of the genre:

Cabaret Mañana — Esquivel (BMG)

Music from a Sparkling Planet — Esquivel (Bar/None)

The In Sounds from Way Out — Perrey & Kingsley (Vanguard)

Sounds of the eras

JAYMZ SAYZ

Going with a theme based on an era? Be sure to look for records with these song titles, most of which you can find recorded by more than one artist.

1920s

"Ain't We Got Fun"

"I'll See You in C.U.B.A."

"Yes, We Have No Bananas"

"Fascinating Rhythm"

1930s

"Minnie the Moocher"

"Cocktails for Two"

"Just a Gigolo"

"On the Sunny Side of the Street"

1940s

"Bali Hai"

"Baby It's Cold Outside"

"That Old Black Magic"

"When I'm Not Near the Girl I Love (I Love the Girl I'm Near)"

1980s

"Steppin' Out"

"Male Curiosity"

"Happy Talk"

1950s

"Ragg Mopp"

"Mambo Italiano"

Theme from "Peter Gunn"

"Baubles, Bangles, and Beads"

1960s

"One Note Samba"

"Music to Watch Girls By"

"Tijuana Taxi"

"Goldfinger"

1970s

"Popcorn"

"The Look of Love"

"Love's Theme"

Theme from *Love Boat*

1990s

"Vertigogo"

"It's Not the End of the World"

"We Are in Love"

"Man Can Fly"

Exotica

Exotica music sends your imagination to some romantic South Sea island. The Polynesian-influenced music was made popular by Yma Sumach, Les Baxter, Martin Denny, and Arthur Lyman.

The legendary Sumach, with her amazing five-octave range, has been an influence on many contemporary singers. Born in Peru, she was originally promoted in the '50s as an Inca princess in direct lineage with the last emperor of the Inca empire. Sumach recorded on Capitol Records.

Les Baxter worked with Sumach for years and created some truly original sounds. Baxter, another exotica guru, penned many classics including "Quiet Villiage," which Martin Denny made famous and put on *Billboard* magazine's U.S. charts in 1957.

In addition to piano, vibes, bass, drums, and unusual Latin percussion instruments, Denny punctuated his style of exotica with bird calls and animal sounds. His 37 albums have seen a resurgence in interest after his music was featured on *Pee Wee's Playhouse;* today, Denny is one of the top-selling artists of this genre.

Examples of the genre:

Xtabay — Yma Sumach (EMI)

The Lost Episode of Les Baxter — Les Baxter (Dionysus)

Afro-Desia — Martin Denny (Rhino)

Exotica Volumes 1 & 2 — Martin Denny (Scamp)

Latin and South American music

Cha cha, salsa, mambo, and bossa nova rhythms, which all originated in different parts of Central and South America, are guaranteed to get the late feeders away from the salad bar. This music has a wide appeal because it is rarely played poorly, plus the grooves are infectious and make people feel sexy.

For the romantics, try some Joao Gilberto. As far as dancing goes, you can't get much better than Sergio Mendez and Brazil '66. Dozens of Latino artists are on Milan records, and great compilation albums can be found on Capitol/EMI. Even Herb Alpert and the Tijuana Brass fall under this category — sometimes.

Examples of the genre:

The Legendary Joao Gilberto — Joao Gilberto (World Pacific)

The Look of Love — Sergio Mendez and Brazil '66 (A&M)

Mondo Mambo! — Perez Prado & His Orchestra (Rhino)

Lounge

Back in the '50s, a musical genre known as "pop instrumentals" or "easy listening music" was very popular. The music made hi-fi's resonate with bongos, glass-shattering brass, and perky xylophones. Lounge can also be used to describe cheesy vocals accompanied by a Hammond organ in a seedy hotel. Images of Bill Murray singing "Star Wars" on *Saturday Night Live,* Rick Moranis doing a laid-back version of "Turning Japanese" on SCTV, or Jerry Lewis as Buddy Love performing "That Old Black Magic" in the original *The Nutty Professor* come to mind.

The term *lounge* (*loungecore* has also been used in recent years) is sometimes used to describe the entire cocktail resurgence, but shouldn't be. Lounge is only one of many types of music under the cocktail umbrella. Unfortunately, few musicians appreciate the title, because lounge singers as a rule are the ones who don't play the bigger rooms. Wayne Newton and Vic Damone may have been considered lounge acts early in their careers, but in no time they were filling rooms and drawing salaries far from the world of lounge.

Examples of the genre:

The Shadow of Your Smile — Friends of Dean Martinez (SubPop)

A Groovy Place — Mike Flowers Pops (Mercury/Polydor)

Cocktails with Joey — Joey Altruda (Will Records)

The Easy Project: 20 Loungecore Favorites — Various Artists (Sequel Records)

Big band swing

Whether you choose an instrumental song by Duke Ellington or a Frank Sinatra crooning tune, you can't go wrong with big band music. Big band got its start during Prohibition in the early '20s and is perhaps the only form of jazz that has always been accessible to the masses, albeit in different forms. Big bands played jitterbug for teenagers in the '40s and went on to play every showroom in Las Vegas in the '50s.

Today, seeing a big band live is a rare treat. Groups tour infrequently because of the costs of setting up such a large show. Harry Connick, Jr. enjoyed great success in the early '90s, but changed to a smaller band with a more roots-oriented New Orleans sound. Tony Bennett also stopped touring with a big band, opting for a small jazz trio instead. Not that Bennett can complain — his last CD, "Here's to the Ladies," is the best-selling record he ever made, and his *MTV Unplugged* received a Grammy for Best Record of the Year award. Jazz music and cocktail parties may go hand in hand, but big band swing is the preferred type of jazz because it keeps the room jumping!

Example of the genre:

Sinatra at the Sands with Count Basie and His Orchestra/ Arranged and Conducted by Quincy Jones (Reprise Record)

Great soundtracks

Soundtracks from groovy movies always have songs worth spinning at a cocktail party. "South American Getaway" from *Butch Cassidy and the Sundance Kid* by Burt Bacharach is a classic! Soundtracks from *Beyond the Valley of the Dolls* or *Austin Powers: International Man of Mystery* have a psyche-delic cocktail quality, and Henry Mancini's *Pink Panther* or *Breakfast at Tiffany's* soundtracks are real crowd pleasers, too!

Pick a Bond film and see if your local record store carries the soundtrack. The soundtrack to *Casino Royale* is smoking from beginning to end, as is the soundtrack to a non-Bond film, *The Party*. More recently, the movie *Swingers* has some choice cuts, and the Jack Lemmon/Walter Matthau movie *Out to Sea* has a hilarious version of "Oy Como Va" by Brent Spiner (also known as Data on *Star Trek*).

Examples of the genre:

Out to Sea — Various Artists (Milan/BMG)

Four Rooms — Combustible Edison (Elektra)

Surf — new and old

Surf music may be derived from rock and roll but, in many cases music by The Ventures, Dick Dale, or Shadowy Men from a Shadowy Planet can give your bash a boost, particularly at an outdoor event. The grooves are much simpler than Latin music, the musicianship doesn't require years of "Scale School," and the production is usually quite straight forward, but despite all of this, surf can sometimes work wonders at cocktail parties.

The key here is to find surf music that is instrumental and not too hard. (The Cramps, for example, are miles away from the cocktail genre of music.)

Examples of the genre:

Dim The Lights, Chill The Ham — Shadowy Men from a Shadowy Planet (Jet Pac/Cargo)

Endless Summer — The Sandals (Tri-Surf Records)

Pulp Surfin' — Various Artists (Del Fi)

Surfing — The Ventures (GNP)

Surf and Drag Volume 1 & 2 — Various Artists (Sundazed Records)

Elevator Music

This style of music, typified by Muzak, is not going to get people dancing at your cocktail party, but it may be desirable during some mellow moments.

Muzak is "Auditory Environmental Architecture" and was developed by a general in the U.S. Signal Corps. Industrial psychologists realized that music could direct work motivation and that boring work gets done faster with fewer mistakes when listening to Muzak, so Muzak was introduced to offices and factories around the time of WWII.

Classic elevator music stylists include: Montovanni, Jackie Gleason Orchestra, Ray Conniff Singers, and Percy Faith. For more specific details on Muzak, I highly recommend the book *Elevator Music* by Joseph Lanza.

Playing the Music

Knowing the different genres of cocktail music still leaves one important musical detail unanswered: how you're going to deliver the sound to your cocktail party guests. Do you want to go all out with a band, hire a DJ, or would you rather play CDs? You have much to consider.

Think about the sound system you need. Size isn't everything. These days you can get amazing sound from a small PA or stereo. Your sound system can be anything from a home stereo to a massive rig, depending on the size of the venue and the amount of people expected. One tip: Have more power than you require. A cocktail party crowd makes noise, so you don't want to discover that the sound system that sounded great before 100 guests showed up can barely be heard after the party starts.

But getting an adequate stereo is the least of your problems. Deciding who is going to play the music or if you include a live band during your party is what takes serious thought.

One thing you don't want to do is play the radio at a cocktail party. No matter how great the programming, at some point a radio station interrupts the music for talk and commercials.

The solo act (playing the music yourself)

If you don't have the space, money, or resources for a DJ or any live entertainment, you can still play CDs or make mixed tapes in advance. Making tapes takes more time and thought than you may think, so if you have friends who are better qualified, ask for their assistance. Just be sure to keep the tapes lively and true to the theme of your party, with perhaps a few surprises. For example, if you have a guest of honor you may want to find out what his or her favorite song is, and slip it in.

If you find yourself alone with a multi-disk CD player, why not fill it with compilation CDs and hit "shuffle" or "random" on the player? Even cocktail aficionados who own the compilation records won't know which song is coming next!

I've given you a list of great records and composers/arrangers in this chapter, and even more in the appendix. If you only have a CD or record player, always remember that you can't go wrong with a Mambo or Cha Cha compilation.

If you are using a turntable for spinning vinyl, be sure to bounce around on the floor and make sure that dancing doesn't make the records skip. Also check that the records you have put aside for the evening are in the right jackets and are not damaged or scratched.

CDs are generally not a problem, but if you're using a new system, or have moved it around, double check quickly to make sure that it isn't damaged. You may wish to clean your CDs with a damp cloth before the party. If you are using a recordable CD (or CDR) — perhaps a compilation from a DJ or a friend's test recording — make sure that it will play in your compact disc player.

Dance to your own drummer

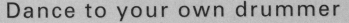

This concept is not exactly a theme party, but it makes for a bizarre home video! Here's the idea:

✔ Ask your guests to bring a personal CD player (a Walkman or Discman) with a set of headphones to the party, along with whatever music they wish to dance to.

✔ At the beginning of your party, play some pleasant background music, then ask your guests to put on their headsets. While they're doing this, switch to a more up-tempo rhythm. The video picks this music up, but your guests are dancing to their own beat!

Hiring a DJ

Professional party consultants agree that a DJ (disc jockey) is almost always better than simply playing CDs, records, or tapes. The trick is to find the right DJ.

It's not rocket science, but the soundtrack that accompanies a great party should be unique and unforgettable. The person who spins these old vinyl classics or selects the CD tracks should really be located in an obvious place at the party, encouraging people to look at his collection and make requests.

How to find your ideal cocktail party DJ:

✔ Go to a local night club or lounge and ask around. If you aren't involved in the cocktail scene in your city, you can usually find an ad for a local club or bar in the newspaper; look for "martini" or "scotch and cigar" theme nights. See what type of clientele the DJ at one such event attracts and check out the record collection the DJ has.

✔ Ask your friends. Chances are someone you know has met a groovy DJ.

No matter who recommends the person, you must sit down live and get to know each other. One person's awesome DJ is another person's nightmare.

✔ As a last resort, look in the Yellow Pages of your phone book. Arrange an appointment to meet the person, explain your needs, and make certain that he has the music required and a pleasant disposition. Most DJ's in the phone book will play everything from Abba to Zappa. Benny Goodman can only follow Madonna at a wedding . . . cocktail DJs are an entirely different thing.

Top five signs you've hired the right cocktail party DJ:

1. He dresses like Austin Powers.

2. When asked to "Play Misty for Me" he inquires: "Which one? I have the Vic Damone, Tony Bennett, and Leonard Nimoy versions."

3. The volume is loud enough for dancing, yet quiet enough to easily make conversation over.

4. He'll put on a few songs in a row so he can dance with others for a moment.

5. He sets up and removes his own gear. You have enough to do without worrying about his DJ equipment.

Top five signs you've hired the wrong cocktail party DJ:

1. When someone requests a song he retorts "Do you go up to Mick Jagger and tell him what song to play next?"

2. He arrives late, and explains: "Sorry, traffic was bad — anyway, only a dozen people are here, so it's no big deal, right?"

3. He's wearing a Nirvana t-shirt and actually smells like teen spirit.

4. He begins the party playing John Tesh, and follows with Yanni and Kenny G.

5. He heads to the bar for a double before he even sets up his equipment.

Musicians and entertainers

You may want to have a live piano player. Maybe you really like a particular small combo. Here's what you need to know about booking a band:

- Different bands and musicians specialize in different styles. Make sure that you've seen them and like them before engaging them for your party. Just because someone's a piano player doesn't mean that she's right for your party.

- You need to book musicians in advance. Three or four months is not out of the question, although chances are you'll only be able to give them three or four weeks. The band or musicians may use a booking agent, but if you see them at a club, ask who the leader is, how much they charge, and who to contact.

- Musicians' fees can run from hundreds to thousands of dollars, depending on who they are, what they do, and how popular they are. Musicians are used to getting paid well for private parties.

- Clarify what the musicians need and who is providing what. A piano player may just need a piano that's in tune (you may have to hire a tuner to come in), but a singer is going to need a sound system. Once hired, work with them on their various space and sound requirements.

Make sure that the sound system they supply (or ask for) is not too big. Some bands have stage and sound requirements that are unreasonable for a small private party.

✔ Clarify how long they are playing. The old-school standard is for a musician to play three or four sets each lasting from 45 minutes to an hour, with fifteen minute breaks in between. A popular band or performer may just do one set, and expect to be paid a sizable fee. This subject needs to be discussed with the individual band.

✔ Double-check and reconfirm. Musicians and entertainers often live tumultuous lives that are subject to last-minute changes.

Be careful about booking live entertainment for your party. Go see a band and make sure that you like them before engaging them for your party. Different bands and musicians specialize in different styles. Because their volume interjects such an overwhelming ambiance to the party, make sure that your entertainers are the right ones. You want entertainment, not irritainment.

Top five qualities in a cocktail party musical act:

1. They are seasoned performers, dress appropriately, and all look very comfortable. (Being inches away from a musician who is terrified of a live audience is like watching your favorite stand-up comic bomb on stage; it is not a pretty sight.)

2. They understand the volume level necessary for all-around enjoyment.

3. They show you a set list before they begin so you know in advance if there is a song you'll want to dance to.

4. They play certain requests, but draw the line way before hippy protest songs and modern grunge music.

5. They leave without a trace. No scratches in the walls or burn holes in your carpet.

Worst five qualities in a cocktail party musical act:

1. Two words: punk rock.

2. They say they can't perform without dry ice and strobe lights, and the party's in your apartment!

3. They arrive late and then won't stop playing.

4. They bring along Tupperware containers to take home leftover hors d'oeuvres, and set up camp at the bar.

5. Not only do they forget to dress for the theme, but they also look as if they haven't bathed in days.

Don't take anyone's word. You are the one hosting the party, and you are responsible for the party's success or failure. If you cannot check out the band at a live performance, ask for a photo and demo tape. If they don't have either, chances are they are not serious enough to consider. If your budget allows, you can always call the local musician's union and get some old pros. For instrumental jazz standards, you can't go wrong with an old union player who has literally and metaphorically "paid his dues." However, should you require something with a bit more personality, ask around at the local clubs to see if there is a new, happening lounge act in town.

Beware the cheese! Cocktail music is on the rise all over the world — but also rising is the number of cocktail imitators who have their tongue planted so firmly in their cheek it's a wonder they can sing at all. A sense of humor is a definite requirement in the cocktail music scene, but if all you're getting is a cheesy comedian posing as a lounge singer, make sure that your guests can stomach it.

Same old thing?
Try something irritaining!

Obviously you want a small band for a small party, but some themes may allow for something more experimental — such as the performance art world of "irritainment."

Irritainment, simply put, is playing a limited number of songs over and over again, only playing different cover versions. Laura Kikauka, Gordon Monahon, and Gordon W. coined the term and performed it at a conceptual party called KBZ 200. Irritainment traces its roots to 1893, when Parisian composer Erik Satie wrote "Vexations," a one-page piano piece that is repeated 840 times over an

18-hour period. Satie conceived the piece as something people could converse over, as background music or *musique d'ameublement* (furniture music) — a radical thought in an era still dominated by classical compositions played to passive audiences.

KBZ 200 has taken musicians to four continents playing different cover versions of the same three songs for 18 hours in "Vexations-style" events. I've had the pleasure of performing at a few of these events. Musical groups and soloists interpret the three songs, and the whole event has a Tiki or Polynesian theme to it.

This may sound completely absurd to you, but irritainment proves an enjoyable and truly unforgettable party, particularly for artists who have experienced all kinds of parties. I remember seeing award-winning actor Sam Neil at a KBZ event (they've been held in New York, Toronto, and throughout Europe) and he was smiling during the whole performance — well not all 18 hours, but a darned long time!

You don't have to be at one of these parties to get a feel for irritainment. KBZ has a CD out, "The Exotic Trilogy — KBZ 200 Vol. 1," although you may have a little trouble finding it. The three songs featured on the disk — "Quiet Village," "Taboo," and "Caravan" — are historically important songs in the Exotica movement. Of course, if you're really ambitious and are creating your own party tape, you can use different cover versions of the same songs.

This successful example does not necessarily mean that performance art is a good idea for your party. In fact, unless your friends are open to bizarre surprises, bad art can kill a good evening.

Part IV
Drinks and Food

The 5th Wave   By Rich Tennant

POPULAR SPORTS DRINKS

The Dennis Rodman

Equal parts:
Blue Curacao
Green Midori
Red Campari
Garnish with
a pierced
navel orange.

A Tyson Punch

-1 jab bitters
-2 hooks cola
-1 bruised
tomato
(pulverized.)
Serve over
cracked ice
in a
broken glass.

The Steinbrenner Uncordial

Add 1 shot cognac
to a 2 oz. cordial
glass. Remove
cognac; put cognac
back in. Remove
cognac; put cognac
back in.

A Gretsky Wallbanger

1 can LaBatts
beer served
on ice.
Garnish with
a maple leaf

©RICHTENNANT

In this part...

True story: I once went to a party where the hostess — a most bountiful woman — suddenly disappeared. A half-hour later, she reappeared, carried on a board by four men. She was all covered in whipped cream and berries, reminiscent of an old Herb Alpert record. You see, *she* was the centerpiece to the hors d'oeuvres tray.

You probably don't want to get quite so personal with what you serve your guests. But what you serve should reflect some personal touches. You want drinks and food that reflect your theme and that bring enjoyment to your guests. Sound tricky? Not really. Just keep reading.

Chapter 8

Tending the Bar

· ·

In This Chapter

▶ Bar policy

▶ Equipment and liquor: Glossary of terms

▶ Selecting the ideal bartender(s)

▶ Mocktails

· ·

1 once threw a party at a small Japanese restaurant in Vancouver, British Columbia. The restaurant had a little stream around the sushi bar, into which the bar normally floated little boats with different kinds of sushi. For our party, however, the boats carried different types of martinis. Talk about man overboard!

You don't have to go quite that far to throw a great party. Regardless of whether yours is a small party at home or a large party, you want your bar to be functional, but not intrusive. To be functional, you need to have a clear idea of the basic decisions behind the bar (your *bar policy*), the equipment and liquor you need, and some idea of the types of drinks you want to serve. Then you, too, will find yourself throwing swimmingly good parties.

Establishing the Rules of the Road

Your bar policy, like everything else with your party, depends on the type of party you're going to throw and your budget. (See Chapter 1.) Some of the decisions include

    ✔ Do you want an open bar or cash bar?

    ✔ Are you going to hire a bartender or do it yourself? (See Chapter 10 for more on hiring a bartender.)

Normally you want to have an open bar at a house party. The host supplies the drinks and mix. Even if you write BYOB (Bring Your Own Booze, or Bring Your Own Beverage) on your invitation, you should have some beverages around for guests who come unprepared.

A cocktail party does not mean that everybody has to drink alcohol, so be sure that you have plenty of soda, juice, and beverages for people who don't drink. You want people to feel welcome and know that they can have a good time without drinking. You also want to have coffee and tea — regular and herbal — for those who do not drink, and to help wake up those who drink too much.

If you are in a club or rented venue, then you usually have a cash bar. On rare occasions (like if you have an unlimited budget), you can foot the entire bill for the bar; otherwise, if your budget allows, having the first couple of drinks free is always a nice idea. Have someone at the door hand guests coupons for the first two drinks.

Offering a couple of free drinks will increase your attendance. Unfortunately, most venues assume that juices and sodas also require coupons, so don't be disappointed if your tickets go for non-alcoholic drinks. Rarely will a venue charge you for coffee, because very few partygoers ever ask for a cup.

Remember, in most cases, you can be held legally responsible for your guests. Keep an eye on their alcohol consumption! If you have under a dozen guests, you may not have a bartender, so you'll have to monitor the drinking. At larger parties, even with punch, you still need to have a smart bartending staff that can pour drinks, keep an eye on the consumption levels, be able to see when enough is enough, and cut people off if necessary. Don't create a situation where you leave the booze unattended for people to serve themselves, or you'll find yourself with some very inebriated guests.

In a BYOB situation, people will invariably bring booze but no mixer. You do not want to run out of mixer.

Essential Equipment

The perfect *cocktail* is a blending of the flavors of three or more ingredients. If the drink has only two ingredients, then it's a *mixed drink*. If a mixer is added, like lemonade, it becomes a *long drink*. Cocktails come in all varieties, but they're usually made with spirits as the base with herbs, spices, fruit juices, and other spirits added.

During Prohibition, the speakeasies concocted strange mixtures to hide the poor quality of the liquor. Today, with all the best spirits available, you want your cocktail to be the most tasty and desirable blend possible. Creating the best cocktails requires not only the right ingredients, but also the right things to mix those ingredients in.

The fundamentals

You've selected a great theme, and you have top-notch decorations; now you need to have the right equipment for your bar. But having the right equipment doesn't necessarily mean spending a great deal of money. First-time hosts can borrow things from a friend or rent easily. In many cases, the professional bartender you hire has his own equipment. If you do buy, get your equipment from a professional catering shop or a bar utensil supply firm.

Following is a list of the minimum equipment required if you wish to do the job properly:

> ✔ **Shaker.** A shaker is basically something that you slosh the drink mixture around in to mix the drink up. A *standard shaker* consists of two cups, usually one of glass (the *mixing glass*) and one of stainless steel, designed to fit mouth-to-mouth. The glasses are good sized — a pint of beer can fit in one of them. You put your drink ingredients in, slosh them back and forth, and then pour them through a strainer into the customer's drink. The proper strainer for a standard shaker is the *Hawthorn strainer,* which looks like a very, very small stainless steel frying pan with holes in it and wire around the edge to snuggle up to the mouth of the mixing glass.

The *capped shaker* is a single cup with a cap and built-in strainer. Unless you have a burning desire to imitate Tom Cruise in *Cocktail,* I'd recommend the capped shaker. It's easier for beginning bartenders to use.

✔ **Corkscrew.** I'm sure that you've had the experience of battling with a corkscrew and trying to scrape and pry the cork out of a bottle. Spend a couple bucks and get a quality corkscrew.

✔ **Blender.** You rarely use a blender at a cocktail party because very few drinks require one. Also, the noise can spoil the ambiance of your party, so I don't use one unless I'm at a big venue. Nonetheless, if you're planning a party with daiquiris, for example, you can't get by without a blender. Just make sure that you have a blender that is designed to crush ice; it should have a "crush" setting.

✔ **Juice extractor and strainer.** Lots of party drinks require fruit juices. The best parties use freshly squeezed juice. You want little pulp and no seeds to make it into your guests' drinks.

✔ **Fruit knife.** Get a knife that's short and sharp.

✔ **Long-handled bar spoon.** This helps you stir drinks.

✔ **Glass cloth.** You don't want to hand your guests a beautiful drink in a spotty glass. Although you may have washed your glasses beforehand, keep a glass cloth handy for last-second polishing.

✔ **Coasters.** Think you can't do much with your coasters? Guess again. Knowing that guests don't usually pay much attention to the coasters, I once threw a treasure hunt at a party and put the clues on the bottom of the coasters. Some of the hints weren't even hints — they were more like fortune cookie sayings, just to add a little confusion to the game and give guests something to talk about!

✔ **Straws.** Get a variety — long, short, and bendy.

✔ **Ice bucket and tongs.** You can either get a cheap plastic bucket with a lid and plastic tongs, or you can find an elegant silver bucket with sterling tongs. (For more on the ice, see the appropriately titled "Ice, ice, baby" section, later in this chapter.)

Other cocktail party essentials

Small details mean everything at a cocktail party. The bar equipment makes for a great drink, but it doesn't make for a great presentation. Putting a little extra thought into things like garnishes, swizzle sticks, and napkins gives your guests something special to take with them from the bar.

Garnishes

A garnish is usually a piece of fruit cut into one of the following shapes:

- ✔ A twist
- ✔ A spiral
- ✔ A wedge
- ✔ A slice

If you're new to the cocktail party scene and are concerned that your guests may notice that you're still mastering the basics, try these imaginative garnishes. They'll give your guests something else to think about while they're having fun.

- ✔ Citrus peels can be cut into various shapes. You can purchase special cutters to do more elaborate shapes.
- ✔ Melon balls, a slice of watermelon, and so on.
- ✔ Paper parasols, plastic monkeys, and so on. Anything goes in today's cocktail scene.
- ✔ Sherbet/Sorbet (lemon or orange): Dissolve 2 cups of sugar in 1 cup of water and simmer in a saucepan for 2 minutes. Add 1 cup of lemon or orange juice and let cool, then freeze. The garnish should have the firm texture of ice cream and taste sweet but tangy.

Maraschino cherries

Here again, we're talking about a cocktail party institution. Nice, plump, and red, maraschino cherries make an attractive addition to many drinks.

Napkins

Cocktail napkins are essential for two important reasons. They serve as a small plate substitute for your hors d'oeuvres, and can double as a coaster or a wipe. Also, cocktail napkins are crucial because plates should not be seen at a traditional cocktail party, although some parties in the genre today use small plates because the hors d'oeuvres are on a table.

Don't mistake a dinner napkin for a cocktail napkin. A cocktail napkin is small and square. A regular napkin is much bigger.

Plan for approximately two to three napkins per person for a three hour party. Any party supply store has cocktail napkins in all different colors and patterns with flags, tropical birds, tropical sun, and so on. Get more than you need.

Don't even think about having a cocktail party without cocktail napkins. But do think about personalizing them. You can get your own rubber stamp made and put your logo on white napkins. Or look around for some of those classic napkins. You know, the ones with the cartoon jokes on them.

Pimento-stuffed olives

Something about a green olive stuffed with a red pimento and skewered with a charming cellophane toothpick really says cocktail party. They make a great embellishment on canapés, too. Some purists may also wish for the small, pitted olives. Best to have both.

You can also find olives stuffed with hot peppers, anchovies, and so on. This type of variety is really only necessary for larger events.

Swizzle sticks

The swizzle originated in the West Indies, where a swizzle stick was the branch of a tropical bush with forked branches on the end. The drinks were *swizzled,* or the branch was twirled rapidly between the palms of the hands. The expensive, commercially purchased swizzle stick is a straight glass rod about five or six inches long; they often have a knob or decoration on one end. The plastic swizzle sticks come as forks, palm trees, sea horses, mermaids, and just about anything else you can imagine.

This accouterment is one that a thrifty host may be inclined to skip. I mean, what good is a swizzle stick? What are they for if not to swizzle? It's very simple, really. Swizzle sticks serve a very important purpose: They give the guest something to remove from his drink and hold. Swizzle sticks are props.

Toothpicks

Don't go spearing your maraschino cherries and your green olives with just any old toothpick. Use the toothpick that says cocktail party. You can find them at any party store, in all kinds of assorted colors to go with your theme. Purchase party toothpicks with flags, little umbrellas, parrots, tiny swords, and myriad other things.

Glassware

The right drink also requires the proper glassware. The cocktail is all about class and looks, and the right glass makes the best visual impact. By carefully following the recipes and using the correct measurements, you will make the right amount of drink. When you pour the drink, it will fit right into the glass.

The glassware is designed for a specific purpose. Take the martini glass, for example. The glass itself should be well-chilled, and by holding the stem, the guest's hand won't warm the drink before it's consumed. That's the reason that stemmed glassware is used for chilled drinks.

Your glassware must be spotlessly clean. Double-check the glasses after washing them. You may have to polish them with a clean glass cloth. If you rent glassware, then wash it again and look it over carefully.

These are the glass styles that have survived the test of time and will always be in fashion.

Glass equals class

Spend a few bucks and rent some martini glasses if you don't have them. Any party rental supply place can supply them. Don't just go for the plastic ones, either. Show some class and go glass. Yes, a few may get lost or broken, but hey, it's a party. If a glass smashes, quickly sweep it up and then ignore it. The host must never make his guests feel uncomfortable or guilty about a wee accident.

The martini glass

You can't have a real cocktail party without martini glasses. Their beautiful curved shape and elegant line is an international statement that says "cocktail." Though the glass itself is quite dainty and feminine in appearance, it also brings to mind the masculine images of James Bond.

The brandy snifter

The wide shape of this glass serves a functional purpose: to give the drinker a chance to appreciate the wonderful aroma of brandy or cognac. Because brandy is more of a late-night drink, you probably won't need a snifter except for upscale parties. But if you do, make sure that you have plenty of good cigars handy!

The champagne flute

This long, slender glass is designed to display the bubbles in your champagne. You're likely to have overflow if you pour champagne too fast. (Similarly, when you open a champagne bottle, release the cork slowly. You don't want to get your guests wet, or hit them with the cork!)

Champagne flutes aren't just designed to show off the bubbles — they're small because the hangover is so large (due to the sugar in the champagne), and because champagne is so expensive.

The highball glass

A large glass, the highball is for traditional mixed drinks or cocktails such as a screwdriver or a zombie. Generous amounts of ice are usually included with any drink served in a highball.

The Irish coffee glass

The Irish coffee glass is one of the few glasses with a handle at a cocktail party, because — of course — you don't want your guests to burn their hands. This glass can also be used to serve any other fancy coffee drink.

The margarita glass

An essential for your South of the Border party; the wide brim of the margarita glass is usually covered with salt. You can also use this glass to serve daiquiris.

No matter what's inside, a margarita glass really screams "cocktail party!" To make your non-drinkers feel more like one of the gang, put their juice drinks in a margarita glass and add several garnishes.

The old-fashioned glass

Drinks served straight-up or on the rocks are often served in an old-fashioned glass. As such, make sure that you have plenty available.

The shot glass

Not only is the shot glass used for measuring, the glass is also used for bar shots (such as tequila) and for other special drinks.

The wine glass

Technically, separate glass styles should be used for red wine, white wine, or sherry. But nowadays you rarely find all three glass styles at any party. The white wine style should suffice at your party. And you have to be extra careful with red wine spills!

The big chill — and other glass treatments

JAYMZ SAYZ Special drinks deserve special presentations — and special preparations. If you're throwing a small party at home or will be having a high guest-to-bartender ratio, you need to think about preparing your glassware before the party. Here are a few tricks you may need:

✔ **Chilled glass.** The martini glass, for example, is always chilled. Find space in a freezer, or throw ice and a little water inside the glasses and let them stand for a minute or so before using.

✔ **Frosted glass.** Some drinks require a frosted glass. Bury some glasses in shaved ice, store them in the refrigerator, or pop them in the freezer for a few minutes.

✔ **Sugar-frosted glass.** The rim of the glass is dampened with an orange or lemon slice and then dipped in fine sugar.

✔ **Salted glass.** The rim of the glass is dampened with a lime or lemon slice and then dipped in salt or — in the case of a Bloody Caesar or Bloody Mary — in salt and pepper.

Ice, ice, baby

Consider ice to be a primary ingredient of your cocktail. Think about it: When a guest puts the drink up to her lips, is she looking at your shoes? No, she's looking at the ice in the glass! And if you want your drinks to be refreshing, they need ice.

Keep these things in mind about your party ice:

✔ **Have plenty of ice.** As a rough guide to use on a hot summer evening, you will need one 6^1/$_2$ pound bag of ice per every four people.

✔ **Have the right kind of ice.** If you're throwing a Beach Party or a party where you're using straws for your drinks, then shaved ice works best. You should use ice cubes for highballs and for any of the classic cocktails that are served on the rocks or in the old-fashioned glass.

✔ **Have clean ice.** If you are planning on making ice by using your own tap water, hold the water up to the light first and make sure that it passes the spot test. If you see thousands of white filaments in suspension, then the ice will be unacceptable in a clear drink, particularly a classic drink like a martini. You'll notice this problem mainly in areas that have hard water, and nothing you do will get rid of it.

Your best bet is to go to a grocery or drug store and purchase purified drinking water to make your ice. If you're at a venue, then check and see what their ice machine looks like. Hopefully, they have one of those new machines that freeze ice very quickly and produce dry, hard, and *clean* (transparent) ice.

✔ **Keep your ice cold.** Duh! You can buy bags of cubed ice, but don't just set it all in your sink or a bowl and let it melt. If you use ice that's been sitting out, it melts too quickly and leaves your guests with watery drinks. You want your ice as cold as possible, so leave the bulk of it in a freezer and just take out a little bit as you need it for drinks. That way, when a guest finishes her drink, she will still have ice in her glass.

Don't have enough refrigeration? Rental stores have all kinds of coolers, including portable ones on wheels for your outdoor party.

Don't use any toy plastic ice cube things unless they're part of a theme like Americana Backyard Barbecue. Don't bother with gimmicks. Just have good ice.

A Quick Look at Liquors

When thinking about the drinks that you want to serve, think about the ingredients that those drinks require. The following is by no means an exhaustive list (which no book can provide), but it will give you some background on bar staples — liquors that are always good to have on hand when company is coming over.

Aperitifs

Aperitifs, such as vermouth or Dubonnet, can be enjoyed on their own before meals or used in cocktails. They can be very pleasant when you don't want much alcohol. Try them on the rocks with a twist of lemon peel.

Beer

Ah, the "B" word. A good bartender would rather be put to work as a mixologist than as a bottle opener. And traditionalists will tell you that beer does not belong at a cocktail party, but the feel of a can of Soporo or the meal found in a Guiness is occasionally an obsession with certain guests. Don't disappoint them. If budget allows, have a small quantity of imported beer hidden in the refrigerator.

Brandy

If you want to sip one of the oldest drinking spirits available, then go with brandy, which is made from the fermented juices of grapes or various fruits. When someone says brandy, she's usually talking about a grape product, but you can find other kinds such as apple brandy. The best brandies are French — armagnac and cognac — but you can also find good German, Spanish, Italian, Portuguese, Greek, and American brandies. The finest brandy is cognac, best after being aged for twenty years.

Champagne

Champagne will always be a popular choice with people. If your event celebrates a very special occasion, you can't go wrong with champagne. Of course, when choosing a champagne, don't cut corners. Cheap sparkling white wine is not the same thing!

Gin

Gin was the main ingredient of the martini of the Roaring Twenties. It's a grain-mash distillate that is redistilled with such aromatics as juniper berries and coriander seed, and is rumored to be the drink least likely to produce hangovers.

Liqueurs

Liqueurs are alcohol with a distillation or infusion of spices, herbs, or fruit. They are great for after-dinner drinking, and are usually sweet. Many different liqueurs are available with almost every flavor imaginable. They include Creme de Menthe, Drambuie, Glava, Tia Maria, Sloe Gin, and — at least in the eyes of some — Southern Comfort.

Punches

The good old punch has been around forever, and is associated with friends and good times. You can find a punch for every season, cold refreshing ones for summer and hot ones for the cold of winter.

If you're expecting quite a few people and feel like you may be understaffed in the bartending department, then a great punch can be a good solution to handling a large crowd. Remember to have a server, however, in order to keep a handle on consumption levels. You want people to have fun, not stare at the ceiling giggling. Drunk and staggering is no way to have a good time — especially for the people who have to deal with the drunks.

Rum

Rum is the liquor of tropical countries, distilled from sugar cane, molasses, and the by-products of sugar manufacture. It comes with the legends of the 1700s — pirates, privateers, buccaneers, and deeds of derring-do; merchant seamen; explorers; and patriots bearing arms. They drank it straight and in large quantities.

Rum is also the liquor of the Southern Islands; you can find numerous fine blends, both heavy and light in body. Rum goes with the sensuous lifestyle of a tropical paradise. It blends beautifully with other liquors, and mixes very well with fruit juices, especially lime.

Sparkling wine

You can't (or shouldn't) try to pass off sparkling wine as champagne, but in many situations that call for champagne in a cocktail, you can use the less expensive wine. The exception to this would be a Champagne Cocktail or a Mimosa.

Tequila

A distillate of the agave plant, you'll need tequila to make margaritas for your South-of-the-Border theme night.

Some — but not all — brands of tequila come with a worm in the bottle. Should you eat the worm? The worm is in the tequila to draw the toxins out. Some people get sick while others claim they get mild hallucinations. I recommend leaving the worm in the bottle. Don't feed it to your iguana!

Vodka

Native to Russia and Poland, vodka is a neutral spirit distilled from grains. Vodka is the spirit you commonly see people toss back straight. Because it's naturally flavorless and odorless, vodka lends itself to mixing well and is the liquor of some of the classic drinks. Popularized by James Bond, who went from regular Smirnoff (Sean Connery) to the mellow Black Label Smirnoff (Pierce Brosnan), vodka makes a great party mixer that you can also substitute in any cocktail made of gin. Various herbs are added and vodka is sold in many different varieties and flavors.

Don't be fooled by hip advertising — take a few friends to a bar and try a taste test of vodkas. How? Order a few vodka martinis, all made exactly the same way, except only the bartender knows which vodka is in which martini, and then see which vodka you prefer. When mixed with soda or juice, any good quality vodka will do.

Whiskey

If you want to celebrate your Scottish heritage, then this is the stuff that they've been making since at least the 15th Century. The three types made in the United States are rye, bourbon, and corn whiskey. You can also find Irish whiskey and Canadian whiskey. Single malt scotch has become hugely popular and is a real crowd-pleaser.

Wine

It's red. It's white. Sometimes it's even rose.

I highly recommend *Wine For Dummies* for details on choosing an appropriate wine. At a cocktail party, you would normally serve a reasonably priced house wine.

Making your own — so to speak

With high-quality photocopiers available nearly everywhere, you can consider personalizing your party. If the house wine doesn't have a label that you're happy with, or if the wine is cheap — assuming you're in a bar — you can always slap your own label on top, hiding the brand names. With hard liquor, leave the labels showing, as people are very fussy about what booze they prefer.

How Much Liquor Do I Need?

The only cocktail party sin greater than running out of ice is running out of liquor. The proper cocktail party host makes his guests feel as though his hospatility has no limit — at least, until the designated ending time for the party.

Plan on approximately two drinks per hour, per person. Table 8-1 should help you determine how much liquor you'll need.

Table 8-1	Table of Party Equivalents	
If You're Entertaining	*Pre-Dinner Cocktails You'll Average*	*For a Party You'll Average*
4 People	8 to 12 Drinks	12 to 16 Drinks
6 People	12 to 18 Drinks	18 to 24 Drinks
8 People	16 to 24 Drinks	24 to 32 Drinks
12 People	24 to 36 Drinks	36 to 48 Drinks
20 People	40 to 60 Drinks	60 to 80 Drinks
25 People	50 to 70 Drinks	75 to 100 Drinks
40 People	80 to 120 Drinks	120 to 160 Drinks

Of course, you'll need different kinds of liquor, because different people will order different things. You will probably find that taste preferences today are (in order) vodka, scotch, and gin. Figure on about 13 two-ounce drinks to a fifth of spirits.

Just so you have extra, use quarts instead of fifths.

If you're serving champagne, figure on six to eight servings from a bottle and about one and a half drinks per guest. One case of champagne (12 fifths) serves 50 people (82 drinks).

If you party with the type of people I do, then multiply the above drink requirements by three, but have designated drivers.

Other Things You Need to Know before Pouring

You have the equipment, you have the liquor, and you're just about ready to pour — but wait. There's a problem. You have a recipe that calls for a dash, a spiral, and a shaking. What does that mean?

This section looks over some of the more common terms you'll run across while preparing for your cocktail party.

Measurements

Whether you are new to mixing drinks or not, always measure each drink; they'll be much more consistent. Here are the terms used in drink recipes:

- Pony — 1 ounce
- Jigger — usually $1^1/_2$ ounces
- Scoop (of ice) — approximately 1 cup
- Splash (of syrup, lemon juice, or grenadine) — $^1/_4$ ounce
- Dash (as of bitters) — $^1/_8$ teaspoon
- Bar spoon or teaspoon — $^1/_8$ ounce
- Pinch — whatever you can get between your two fingers

Make each drink carefully, as if it's the first and last one you'll ever make. If you don't appreciate the art of the fine cocktail, then hire a bartender who does.

The terms

Bartenders use the English language; they just use it in a way that's different from everyday speech. So that you have an idea of what a bartender or a drink recipe is talking about, take a look at these terms:

- **Add:** Combine into the drink or vessel. Where appropriate, mix gently with a bar spoon. The current trade jargon is *build* when adding ingredients directly to a serving glass in this way.

- **Blend:** Blend and pour unstrained.

- **Broken ice:** Large cubes chopped down to about one-third the original size (also known as *bar ice*).

- **Frosted:** Glass sufficiently chilled in the fridge or freezer, or by filling the glass with crushed ice, to form a cold mist on the outside.

- **Garnish:** Decorate or attach to the rim of the glass.

- **Ignite:** Set on fire.

- **Long:** A total of five measures or more of fluid.

- **Mix:** To combine the ingredients, usually by using a bar spoon. When you mix a drink, you must stay with the recipe. Some drinks need to be shaken; others need to be stirred. This has to do with the blending of the ingredients; shaking is crucial for hard-to-blend ingredients. Don't interchange the two techniques or you will spoil the drink.

- **Pour:** To add to the glass without straining, unless specified.

- **Pousse-café:** Add the ingredients (minimum of three) over a bar spoon in order of density so as to form distinct layers in the glass. Use a straight-sided glass This is really a style of presentation.

- **Rim:** Coat the rim of the glass by moistening and then dipping into the specified dry material such as powdered sugar or salt.

- **Shooter:** Usually downed in one gulp.

- **Short:** Less than five measures of fluid in total before making the drink.

- **Smooth:** When blended with ice, mixture achieves the consistency of a thick milkshake.

> ✔ **Spiral:** Long, coiled, virtually pith-free length of citrus peel.
>
> ✔ **Strain:** To pour out, leaving the ice and other solids behind. If you have stirred the drink, then use a Hawthorn strainer.
>
> ✔ **Twist:** 1^1/$_4$- to 2^1/$_2$-inch (3–6 cm) length of pith-free citrus peel, held over the drink and twisted in the center to release a little essential oil onto the surface. Add twist to drink unless otherwise stated.

Shaken or stirred?

The general rule is that all drinks made with clear ingredients should be stirred with ice, and those made with fruit juices should be shaken. The harder the shake, the colder and better the drink is. Of course Bond prefers his martini shaken, and who is going to argue with a man with a license to kill? I also enjoy the extra cold and misty effect achieved from shaking.

Shaking is done in a mixing glass, stirring is done with a spoon. Avoid using a blender — they lack class and can be messy. For some punches or drinks that contain fruit, milk, eggs, or cream, you will need an electric mixer. You'll also need one if you make daiquiris (which are hard to make properly) or drinks that require snow ice.

Shaking

Drinks containing eggs, fruit juices, or cream are shaken. The object is to freeze the drink while breaking down and combining the ingredients.

To *shake and strain,* fill up your shaker half way with whole ice cubes, add the ingredients, and shake briskly until the exterior of the vessel is very cold. Pour the drink immediately through the built-in strainer or Hawthorn strainer, filling up the glassware and leaving the ice in the shaker. Because you're adding ice to the ingredients and some of it will melt, the amount of liquid being poured does increase.

If you're pouring a drink that specifies "shake and pour unstrained," then add the recipe and a glassful of ice to the shaker, cover the top, and shake. A *Boston shaker* (which keeps the ice separate from the actual drink, kind of like an ice cream freezer keeps the ice away from the ice cream) comes in handy here, as this technique ensures that the total volume of the drink doesn't increase, no matter how much of the ice melts.

If you have shaken two or three of the same drinks together at once, line up the glasses and pour each drink halfway. Then go back and top them all off. Doing so keeps their contents consistent.

Stirring

Stirring is primarily for drinks made up of clear ingredients. The object is to chill and thoroughly mix the ingredients while retaining the clear clarity.

To *stir and strain,* fill half of a mixing glass or the bottom half of a shaker with ice cubes, add the ingredients, and stir the drink quickly with a long-handled bar spoon for 15 to 20 seconds. Put a Hawthorn strainer on top and pour out the liquid into the proper serving glass.

If the recipe calls for "stir and pour unstrained," then mix the drink the same way, but use only one glassful of ice and do not strain the liquid. Pour the entire contents into the same size glass that you measured the ice with.

Are pre-mixes okay?

Many pre-mixed drinks are available in both liquid and powdered form. Making drinks such as sours, gimlets, and Manhattans is easy, so don't use pre-mixes. When it comes to more exotic drinks like Mai Tais and piña coladas, try them and see what you think. Pre-mixes may be a better idea with these kinds of drinks.

Many prepared nonalcoholic mixes are on the market today, both for commercial use and for the home. They're usually good, they're consistent, and they speed things up. Use them. Without liquor added, you can use many of them to make non-alcoholic smartinis (discussed in the last section in this chapter) as well.

Other tips for new bartenders

When you're mixing a drink, put the cheaper ingredients in first. That way, if you make a mistake, you haven't wasted the more expensive liquor. You may find the following tips helpful as well:

- ✔ Never shake the fizzy drinks.

- ✔ Keep things cold. Store all your mixers in the refrigerator ready to be put in the cocktail right before serving.

- ✔ Place the ice in the shaker or glass before you add the liquor. That way, you start the process of cooling the drink right from the start.

- ✔ When you blend a cocktail with crushed ice, you're trying to produce a consistency that is not unlike that of a milkshake. Don't use crushed ice in a shake and strain drink. Drinks that are shaken with crushed ice are always intended to be poured unstrained.

- ✔ If you mix a cocktail containing cream, you need to wash the shaker out more thoroughly than with other drinks. The cream sticks to the inside of the shaker and taints the next noncream drinks.

- ✔ Fresh ingredients are best. Fruit should be freshly sliced, and fruit juices just squeezed. If you don't have the time, use only frozen lemon and orange juice for your drinks; stay away from artificial beverages.

- ✔ Use high-quality, branded products.

- ✔ Many of the recipes can be made in quantity and left in the fridge until the guests arrive, but any drink containing cream or eggs cannot — they will separate and curdle. If you pre-mix drinks, do not add the ice until you are serving.

- ✔ Many seasoned drinkers will want their cocktails strong — more spirits and less flavoring. People new to drinking itself — or trying to make it through a long night — will want them lighter. A knowledgeable bartender can cater to the individual by altering the potency to fit the drinker.

- ✔ For a summer party, you can experiment with gelatin cubes. Substitute vodka in place of $1/4$ to $1/2$ the water, and chill as directed.

- ✔ In general, cocktails should be served ice cold, although some winter mixed drinks and grogs are served hot.

A cocktail is a minor work of art — usually at its peak of appeal when just poured — which should be pleasing to the eye as well as to the palate. To create a pleasant mood of anticipation for your guest, remember to smile when shaking. And stand with perfect posture when presenting the finished drink.

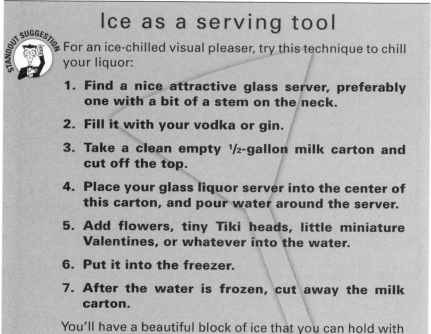

Ice as a serving tool

For an ice-chilled visual pleaser, try this technique to chill your liquor:

1. **Find a nice attractive glass server, preferably one with a bit of a stem on the neck.**

2. **Fill it with your vodka or gin.**

3. **Take a clean empty ½-gallon milk carton and cut off the top.**

4. **Place your glass liquor server into the center of this carton, and pour water around the server.**

5. **Add flowers, tiny Tiki heads, little miniature Valentines, or whatever into the water.**

6. **Put it into the freezer.**

7. **After the water is frozen, cut away the milk carton.**

You'll have a beautiful block of ice that you can hold with a towel and serve the liquor from.

The Classic Drinks

Hundreds of drinks have been invented over the years, and most of the new drinks with crazy names are just slight variations of an old standby. Only a few cocktails have survived the decades to become cocktail party standards. Practice your bartending skills on a few friends over a long period of time. I say this not only because I can't condone drinking to excess — as in "I practiced bartending all night" — but also because someone who's inebriated isn't fit to judge a good drink.

A drink is more than just a recipe. Two bartenders can follow the same recipe and get a slightly different drink. You may find that you can make one drink very well and another not so well.

The following cocktail drinks are grouped together by the basic liquor used. All of the recipes that I've mentioned will

work at any of the various parties you may put on, but refer
back to the theme listings in Chapters 3 and 4 for certain
matchups that work especially well. And for more recipes,
see *Bartending For Dummies,* by Ray Foley (published by IDG
Books Worldwide, Inc.).

Cocktail

Basic liquor plus bitters, vermouth, and other flavors. A
cocktail is always served cold.

Bloody Caesar

1¹/₄ oz.	Vodka	Pour vodka into a glass with ice
2¹/₂ oz.	Clamato juice	and fill with clamato juice. Add
dash	Worcestershire sauce	a dash of tabasco, worcestershire,
dash	Tabasco sauce	pepper, and salt. Garnish with a
dash	Salt and pepper	celery stalk or a lime wheel.

A popular drink in Canada.

Gibson

2 oz.	Dry gin	Stir with ice. Add cocktail
Dash	Martini & Rossi	onion. Serve straight up
	Extra dry vermouth	or on ice.
	Cocktail onion	

Gimlet

1¹/₄ oz.	Vodka	Mix vodka and lime juice in a
¹/₂ oz.	Fresh lime juice	glass with ice. Strain and serve
		in a cocktail glass. Garnish
		with twist of lime.

You can also serve this one on ice in a highball glass.

Gin & Tonic

1¹/₄ oz.	Gin	In a glass fllled with ice, add gin
	Tonic	fill with tonic. Add a lime wedge.

Manhattan

	2 oz.	American or Canadian whiskey	Stir. Garnish with a cherry.
	Splash	Sweet or dry vermouth	
	Dash	Angostura Bitters	

Martini

	2 oz.	Vodka or gin	Shake or stir vodka or gin and vermouth over ice. Strain and serve in a cocktail glass straight up or over ice. Garnish with a twist or an olive.
	Dash	Extra dry vermouth	

Rob Roy

	2 oz.	Scotch	Stir over ice and strain.
	Dash	Sweet or dry vermouth	

A classic cocktail. You can also serve it with ice.

Coffee

A highbrow cocktail party needs to serve good coffee. If you're not a coffee drinker, or are unfamiliar with designer coffee, go with a French or Vienna Roast. People who love their coffee love it dark; if you can see the bottom of the cup, it's tea. One-and-a-half heaping tablespoons of grounds per cup of water should do it. Don't leave the coffee on the burner all night. Make a new pot every couple of hours.

One pound of coffee serves 60 to 80 cups. Remember, if you are having a large party and are renting a large coffee urn, the coffee can take up to an hour to brew.

Collins

Spirits (usually gin, whiskey, rum, or brandy), sugar, and soda water.

John Collins

1 oz.	Bourbon or whiskey	Pour lemon juice, syrup, and Whiskey in a highball glass filled with ice. Squeeze in the juice from 1/2 lime and save the shell. Fill the glass with club soda. Stir. Decorate with used lime.
1/2 oz.	Sugar syrup	
	Juice of 1/2 Lime	
	Club soda	
	Lemon juice	

This is Tom's brother.

Tom Collins

1 1/2 oz.	Gin	Shake first two ingredients and pour over ice. Top with over ice. Top with club soda.
	Juice of 1 lemon	
	Club soda	

Cooler

A summer drink — long and iced. A cooler is made with a basic liquor or sherry, port, or wine; lemon; sugar; and soda water, with ice.

Cafe Cooler

1/2 oz	Romana sambuca	Pour coffee over ice. Add Sambuca and half & half. Add Half & Half. Add brown sugar to taste.
5 oz.	Coffee	
1/2 oz.	Half & half	
Dash	Brown sugar	

Colosseum Cooler

1 oz.	Romana sambuca	Combine sambuca and cranberry juice in a tall glass. Fill with soda and garnish with a lime wedge.
3 oz.	Cranberry juice	
	Club soda	

Mint Cooler

1 oz.	Bombay gin	In a tall glass with ice, combine the first two ingredients. Fill glass with club soda.
1/4 oz.	Peppermint schnapps	
	Club soda	

Flip

Whole egg with whiskey, apple brandy, cognac, or rum in a blender.

Frappe

Pouring drink over cracked ice.

Baileys Coconut Frappe

2 parts	Baileys Irish Cream	Shake or blend until frothy;
1 part	Malibu rum	pour over ice and garnish
2 parts	Milk	with toasted coconut.

You can also serve this one in a cocktail glass.

Highball

Spirits served with ice, ginger ale, soda water, or colas.

Highball

1½ oz.	Canadian or American whiskey	Combine and stir.
3 oz.	Ginger ale	

Hawaiian Highball

3 oz.	Irish whiskey	Combine the whiskey with
2 tsp.	Pineapple juice	juices. Add ice and fill with
1 tsp.	Lemon juice	soda. Stir gently.
	Club soda	

Long Island Iced Tea

½ oz.	Vodka	Shake first five ingredients
½ oz.	Rum	over ice and strain into a
½ oz.	Gin	and strain into a highball
½ oz.	Triple Sec	glass. Fill with cola.
½ oz.	Tequila	
	Cola	

Many variations exist.

Julep

Fresh mint and bourbon whiskey.

Mint Julep

2 oz.	Makers Mark bourbon	In a silver cup, mash 4 mint leaves with sugar sypup. Fill cup with crushed ice. Add bourbon and garnish with a mint leaf.
¹/₄ oz.	Sugar syrup (sugar/hot water)	
5	Mint leaves	

Don't forget that it's served in a silver cup.

Punch

Hot or cold, usually with fruit and sugar, combined in spirits or wine. One gallon of punch serves approximately 24 persons. (32 three-ounce drinks with ice.)

If a recipe calls for a half a lemon and you're using bottled lemon juice, be careful about overdoing it. Too much lemon can ruin a drink.

If the punch recipe calls for champagne, you can substitute sparkling wine. If you choose to serve a punch, be sure to have an alcohol-free option nearby, because some people will be anxious about the unknown potency of a bowl full of punch.

Unless you know a punch recipe by heart, I recommend that you cut back on all your ingredients except ice by 15 to 20 percent. Mix it up, try it, and then season to your taste. Be careful with the ice, have plenty on hand, but don't put it all in the punch. Have some available so that you can add a little more to the individual glass when you serve it.

Make your punch a few hours before your party so the ice has time to dilute into it. If you have to mix it up right at the party, then dilute your punch a bit with some cold soda.

Put your punch into any container large enough that you can clean and fill.

Ambrosia Punch

20 oz. can	Crushed pineapple, undrained	In blender container, puree pine-
15 oz.	Coco Lopez cream of coconut	apple and cream of cocunt until
2 cups	Apricot nectar, chilled	smooth. In punch bowl, combine
2 cups	Orange juice, chilled	the pureed mixture, nectar, juice,
1½ cups	Light rum, optional	and rum (if desired). Mix well.
1 liter	Club soda, chilled	Just before serving, add club soda
		and serve over ice.

Bacardi Confetti Punch

750 ml.	Bacardi light rum	Combine the first four ingredients
6 oz. can	Frozen lemonade concentrate	in a large container and chill for
6 oz. can	Frozen grapefruit juice	two hours, stirring occasionally.
	concentrate	To serve, pour the mixture over
6 oz. can	Fruit cocktail, drained	ice in a punch bowl and add 2 liters
2 liters	Club soda, chilled	of chilled Club Soda. Stir gently.

Champagne Punch Royale

1 bottle	Chantaine sparkling wine,	Place sliced strawberries in large
	chilled	bowl and sprinkle with sugar.
⅓ cup	Royale Montaine cognac and	Add orange juice and cognac and
	Orange liqueur	orange liquor. Macerate for 1 hour.
1 cup	Sliced strawberries	Add chilled sparkling wine and
1 cup	Orange juice	club soda.
1 small	Club soda	
bottle		
2 Tbsp.	Sugar	

Malibu Party Punch

1 bottle	Malibu	Combine ingredients in a punch
48 oz.	Cranberry juice	bowl and stir. Garnish with
6 oz. can	Frozen orange juice	lemon, orange slices, and cloves.
	concentrate	
6 oz. can	Frozen lemonade or limeade	
	concentrate	

M&R Hot Spiced Wine Punch

1500 ml	Martini & Rossi red vermouth	Combine all ingredients except
2 dashes	Angostura bitters	orange slices in a heavy saucepan
6	Cloves	and heat, but don't boil. Strain
3	Cinnamon sticks	into a punch bowl. For added
3 tsp.	Superfine sugar	effect, heat a poker and dip it into
pinch	Allspice	the punch before serving. Garnish
pinch	Ground clove	with orange slices.
	Orange slices	

Open House Punch

750 ml.	Southern Comfort	Chill ingredients. Mix first 4
6 oz	Lemon juice	ingredients in punch bowl. Add
6 oz. can	Frozen lemonade	7-Up or Sprite. Add drops of red
6 oz. can	Frozen orange juice	food coloring as desired and
	concentrate	stir. Garnish with orange and
3 liters	7-Up or Sprite	lemon slices. Note that the first 4
	Red food coloring	ingredients may be mixed in
		advance. Add 7-Up or Sprite and
		ice when ready to serve.

Sling

Spirits (usually gin, rum, and whiskey) poured over ice, dissolved sugar, lemon juice, and bitters.

Bourbon Sling

2 oz.	Bourbon	In a shaker half-filled with ice
1 tsp.	Superfine sugar	cubes, combine the sugar, water,
2 tsp.	Water	lemon juice and bourbon. Shake
1 oz.	Lemon juice	well. Strain into a Collins glass.
		Garnish with a lemon twist.

Irish Sling

1 oz.	Tullamore Dew	Crush sugar with ice in a glass.
1 oz.	Gin	Add Tullamore Dew and gin. Stir.
1 lump	Sugar	

Raffles Bar Sling

1/4 oz.	Benedictine	Combine gin, bitters, lime juice,
3/4 oz.	Gin	and cherry-flavored brandy with ice
1/4 oz.	Cherry-flavored brandy	ice in a highball glass. Stir in ginger
2 dashes	Bitters	beer. Float Benedictine on top.
1/2 tsp.	Lime juice	Garnish with mint.
	Ginger beer	

Singapore Sling

1 1/2 oz.	Gin	Shake first five ingredients and
1/2 oz.	Cherry-flavored brandy	pour into a tall glass. Top with
3 dashes	Benedictine	with club soda.
Dash	Rose's grenadine	
Dash	Sweetened lime mix	
	Club soda	

Sour

Spirits shaken with lemon or lime juice and sugar (often with the white of an egg).

Apricot Sour

2 Tbs.	Lemon juice	Combine all ingredients except
1/2 tsp.	Superfine sugar	the 1/2 slice of lemon in shaker
2 oz.	Apricot brandy	of lemon in shaker and shake
3-4	Ice cubes	igorously. Strain into a chilled
		cocktail glass. Garnish with lemon.

The hot drink of the '60s.

Scotch Sour

1 1/4 oz.	Scotch	Stir ingredients in a mixing glass
1 oz.	Lemon juice	and pour into a rocks glass with
1 tsp.	Sugar	ice. Garnish with a cherry and an
		orange slice.

Sours can be made with any liquor. You can also shake this drink with cracked ice.

Whiskey Sour

1½ oz.	Seagram's V.O.	Shake with ice. Serve straight
¾ oz.	Sweetened lemon juice	up or over ice.
1 tsp.	Superfine sugar	

Toddy

Spice (cinnamon, clove, nutmeg, and lemon peel) in a glass with a spirit, and hot water.

Hot Toddy

1 ½ oz.	Seagram's V.O.	Pour Seagram's into hot water.
1 lump	Sugar	Add sugar and cloves. Stir.
2	Cloves	
	Hot Water	

Smartinis and Mocktails — Smart Cocktails

Many people today are either on a twelve-step program or reducing their intake of alcohol for health reasons. That doesn't mean that they don't want to drink anything, and many of these people will be the liveliest and most fun to have at your party. Other guests will be drinking alcohol, but will want to rotate with *mocktails* — a cocktail without the alcohol — or a smartini — water with a twist — so they can go all night and then drive home. Make sure that those guests aren't stuck drinking humdrum pop or club soda.

You're going to need to make sure that your bartender is just as adept at alcohol free drinks as the classic cocktails. Almost any regular cocktail can be a tasty treat by simply eliminating the booze. Virgin Caesars, Marys, Daiquiris, and so on. Adding imaginative garnishes makes the drink look like a regular cocktail.

I live off smartinis. I usually have a few martinis in an evening, and all the rest of the time I have smartinis. It gives the impression that I am partying wildly but guarantees that I will be in shape for the evening and also doubles as hangover prevention.

Chapter 9

Tasty Tidbits

*Y*ou can't have a true cocktail party without breaking bread, so you have to have something on a table when people arrive or have food served by a waiter or waitress after all of your guests are present. You don't have to serve a big meal, but it should look lovely. You can serve hors d'oeuvres that are gone in the first hour or two of the party, but you should serve something more imaginative than chips and pretzels.

Hors d'oeuvres reflect the personality of the host, so if you don't feel confident in reflecting your personality with anything other than a bag of chips, make sure that you delegate this task to someone or hire a caterer. Even if you're throwing an intimate cocktail party for a dozen friends, at least have spiral sandwiches or little treats.

Hors d'oeuvres means "outside the work," so the term literally means that the food should stimulate enthusiasm for what is to follow. Hors d'oeuvres sometimes usher in a meal, but they are not meant to be a meal in themselves. At a cocktail or theme party, the finger food should reflect the same attitude as the overall party. When pondering your food choices, always think about the theme of your party. If you're putting on a sophisticated party, then your hors d'oeuvres should be elegant. If you're putting on a crazy theme party, then go a little crazy with the finger food.

What Hors d'Oeuvres Should I Have?

The choice is yours, but I've given you suggestions for each of the different theme parties. *Cooking For Dummies* by Bryan Miller and Marie Rama, *Desserts For Dummies* by Bryan Miller and Bill Yosses, *Gourmet Cooking For Dummies* by Charlie Trotter, or *Lowfat Cooking For Dummies* by Lynn Fischer (all published by IDG Books Worldwide, Inc.) can give you more ideas. But keep in mind these two suggestions when you are deciding on hors d'oeuvres:

- If you have hot hors d'oeuvres, they should be followed with cold ones.
- If you have a crisp and chewy selection, then have a soft and unctuous one as well.

Whatever you do, make sure that your food can be eaten with one hand. Don't subject your guests to plates or forks — that is not a cocktail party. A cocktail party means a drink in one hand and a small, self-contained tidbit that can be eaten in one bite in the other. Remember, your guest is also standing and chatting while drinking and eating, so don't serve food that's too crumbly, sticky, or messy.

What Are the Common Cocktail Party Hors d'Oeuvres?

The classic hors d'oeuvres that are time-tested and sure to go fast are

- Chilled shrimp with cocktail sauce
- Spinach in wee filo pastry
- Canapés — often smoked salmon

The key here is delicious. I'm not talking about health food; I'm talking about tiny bite-size morsels of food that taste so good that they can't possibly be all that good for you.

Here is a quick look at the most popular kinds of cocktail party hors d'oeuvres, along with some sample recipes. For more recipes, again, see the books mentioned earlier.

Canapés

If you really want to say cocktail party with your snacks, then make sure that you have a tray with canapés as hors d'oeuvres. Making canapes is a fun way to spend the morning before the party.

A canapé (KAH-na-pay) is any hors d'oeuvre that sits on a cracker or a little piece of bread or pastry. It can be anything from a cracker with herb butter and shrimp to a home-baked tiny tart. If bread is used, it's usually covered with flavored butter or some kind of spread and then seasoned with succulent tidbits. A traditional canapé base is a little square of bread that's buttered and slipped under the broiler to form a crispy base.

Olive and Pecorino Cheese Tapenade on Toasted French Bread

People always associate olives with cocktails anyway, so this *tapenade* (olive paste) recipe from *Gourmet Cooking For Dummies* will fit right into any elegant party. The olive and cheese mixture will keep in the refrigerator for at least a week, so pull it out for those pop-in guests.

Preparation time: *15 minutes*

Cooking time: *10 minutes*

Yield: *8 slices*

$1^1/_2$ cups pitted Calamata olives (or any other black Greek olives)

$1^1/_2$ cup grated pecorino cheese (or Parmesan)

2 tablespoons olive oil

8 slices French bread

1 To make the tapenade, finely chop the Calamata olives and toss with the grated cheese.

2 Brush the slices of French bread with the olive oil and toast in the oven until lightly golden-brown.

3 Spread some of the chopped olive and cheese tapenade on top of each slice of bread and serve at room temperature.

Garlic and Goat Cheese Tartines

Tools: *Toaster oven (optional), bread knife*

Preparation time: *About 10 minutes*

Cooking time: *Less than a minute*

¹/₂ loaf French or Italian bread, sliced into ¹/₄-inch (6-mm) pieces

3 cloves garlic, peeled and split

¹/₄ cup (50 ml) olive oil (about)

Salt and freshly ground pepper to taste

8 ounces (250 g) fresh goat cheese

3 sprigs fresh rosemary, thyme, or sage, coarsely chopped

1 In a toaster oven or preheated 400°F (22°C) oven, toast the bread slices until they just begin to turn golden, no more. Let the bread cool.

2 Rub the bread on both sides with the garlic. Drizzle about ¹/₂ teaspoon (2 ml) olive oil over one side of each slice. Lightly salt and pepper the same side.

3 Spread goat cheese over the slices and garnish with chopped fresh herbs.

Yield: *6 to 8 servings.*

Source: *Cooking For Dummies*

Casseroles

Casseroles aren't normal cocktail party fare, but someone is bound to try serving one at a party. Ideally, the casserole is cut into fairly small pieces so the guests can skewer them easily.

Casseroles are a staple of middle-American entertaining. After all, what makes you think more of Mom than meat loaf? This lower-fat version (made with a turkey-beef mix) from *Cooking For Dummies* can be sliced into little squares and served with toothpicks and ketchup or steak sauce.

Beef and Turkey Meat Loaf

Tools: *Chef's knife, medium skillet, large mixing bowl, 5- to 6-cup (1.25-to 1.5-l) loaf pan*

Preparation time*: About 30 minutes*

Baking time: *About 1¹/₂ hours, plus 10 minutes standing time*

2 tablespoons (30ml) olive oil

1 cup (250 ml) peeled and chopped onion, about 1 large onion

1 tablespoon (15 ml) peeled and chopped garlic, about 3 large cloves

³/₄ cup (175 ml) milk

2 eggs

1¹/₂ cups (375 ml) fresh bread crumbs

1 pound (500 g) ground turkey

1 pound (500 g) lean ground beef

2 tablespoons (30 ml) chopped fresh thyme, or 2 teaspoons (10 ml) dried

2 tablespoons (30 ml) chopped fresh savory, or 2 teaspoons (10 ml) dried

2 tablespoons (30 ml) chopped fresh parsley

¹/₄ teaspoon (1 ml) ground nutmeg

Salt and freshly ground pepper to taste

1 Preheat the oven to 350°F (180°C).

2 Heat the oil in a medium skillet over medium heat. Add the onion and cook, stirring, for about 3 minutes or until the onion begins to wilt. Add the garlic and cook, stirring, about 2 minutes more. Do not let the garlic brown. Remove the pan from the heat and set aside.

3 In a large bowl, beat together the milk and eggs, stir in the bread crumbs, and let stand for 5 minutes. Add the remaining ingredients and the sautéed onion and garlic. Combine the mixture thoroughly by using your hands or a wooden spoon.

4 Mold the mixture into a 5- to 6-cup (1.25- to 1.5-l) loaf pan. Bake, uncovered, about 1¹/₂ hours, draining off any excess grease every 30 minutes. Let the meat loaf stand for about 10 minutes at room temperature before slicing.

Yield: *6 meal-sized servings.*

Another perfect backyard or Western-theme treat is baked beans. Combine drained navy beans, molasses, mustard, onions, garlic, green peppers, and tomato sauce and bake, covered, for 1 hour.

Another mom-food favorite:

Kraft Macaroni and Cheese

Follow the directions on the box and add more butter than they say. Don't forget that your guests deserve a special treat, so use a few extra packs of the cheese mixture or add some real grated cheese.

Chicken, Ribs, and Other Meat

Can you say "napkins"? Serve any of these and you'll be best friends with your local paper products sales representative.

But chicken and ribs have their place at cocktail parties because people like them. Just make sure that you get good quality meat.

Crispy Curried Chicken Dumplings with Date Dipping Sauce

Here is a twist on the traditional pot sticker from *Gourmet Cooking For Dummies*. The sweetness of the date helps to tone down the heat of the curry.

Yield: 12 dumplings

3 cups chicken stock (see Gourmet Cooking For Dummies*)*

2 tablespoons curry powder

1 chicken breast, skin removed

¹/₄ cup golden raisins, chopped

¹/₂ cup chopped green onions

Salt and freshly ground black pepper

1 cup dried dates, pits removed

Two 3-inch round won ton skins

1 egg yolk, mixed with 2 table-spoons water

3 tablespoons butter

1 Place the chicken stock in a small saucepan with 1¹/₂ tablespoons of curry powder and simmer over medium heat for 3 minutes. Add the chicken breast and poach for 10 minutes or until the chicken is cooked.

(continued)

2 Remove the chicken (reserve ¹/₂ cup of the cooking liquid) and pull apart into small pieces. Place the pulled chicken in a small bowl and toss with the chopped raisins, green onions, and remaining 1¹/₂ tablespoon of curry powder. Season to taste with salt and pepper.

3 Place the dried dates in a small saucepan with the reserved cooking liquid. Simmer over medium heat for 3 minutes or until the dates have been rehydrated. Puree the dates in the blender and pass through a fine-mesh sieve. Season to taste with salt and pepper.

4 Lay the won ton skins flat and brush half of the edge with the egg yolk mixture. Place some of the chicken mixture in the center of each won ton and fold in half. Press firmly to create a seal.

5 Cook the won tons in boiling salted water for 2 to 3 minutes or until tender.

6 Sauté the cooked dumplings in a hot pan with the butter for 2 to 3 minutes on each side or until golden brown and crispy.

7 Serve with the date sauce.

Source: *Gourmet Cooking For Dummies*

Grilled Brochettes of Pork with Rosemary

Tools: *Chef's knife, mixing bowl, wooden or metal skewers*

Preparation time: *About 25 minutes, plus time to preheat grill*

Marinating time: *About 30 minutes*

Grilling time: *About 20 minutes*

1¹/₄ pounds (625 g) lean boneless pork loin, cut into 1-inch (2.5-cm) cubes

2 tablespoons (30 ml) olive oil

2 tablespoons (30 ml) chopped fresh rosemary, or 2 teaspoons (10 ml) dried

1 tablespoon (15 ml) red wine vinegar

1 teaspoon (5 ml) peeled and finely chopped garlic, about 1 large clove

1 teaspoon (5 ml) ground cumin

¹/₄ teaspoon (1 ml) red pepper flakes

Salt and freshly ground pepper to taste

Vegetable oil for oiling grill grate

(continued)

1 Place the pork in a mixing bowl. Add the remaining ingredients and mix well. Cover with plastic wrap and allow to marinate in the refrigerator for at least 30 minutes.

2 Preheat a charcoal fire or gas grill.

3 Arrange the pork cubes on four skewers. If you use wooden skewers, soak them for half an hour in cold water and cover the tips with foil to prevent burning.

4 Place the meat on a grate that you have lightly brushed with oil. Grill about 4 inches (10 cm) from the fire for about 20 minutes or until done, turning often. Remove the meat from the skewers and serve immediately with toothpicks.

Source: *Cooking For Dummies*

Braised Spare Ribs with Honey and Chipotle Peppers

You can use these tender spare ribs from *Gourmet Cooking For Dummies* to make killer leftover pulled-pork sandwiches. But if you can't wait for them to cool to pull the meat, dig in and serve these ribs with potato wedges.

Preparation time: *15 minutes*

Cooking time: *2 hours and 15 minutes*

Yield: *6 to 8 meal-sized servings*

1 cup chopped onion	*¹/₄ cup honey*
¹/₂ cup chopped celery	*3 chipotle peppers*
¹/₂ cup chopped carrots	*¹/₄ cup molasses*
2 tablespoons vegetable oil	*¹/₂ cup brown sugar*
20 baby back ribs (about 5 pounds)	*¹/₂ chopped cilantro*
Salt and pepper	*2 tablespoons white peppercorns*
¹/₂ cup chopped leeks	*8 cups chicken stock or beef stock*
1 red bell pepper, chopped	

1 Place a large roasting pan over two of your stove burners and caramelize the onion, celery, and carrots with the oil.

(continued)

2 Season the ribs with salt and pepper. Place on top of the caramelized vegetables and roast in the oven at 450°F for 15 minutes.

3 Add the remaining ingredients and cover. Lower the temperature to 300°F and continue to cook the ribs for 2 hours or until the meat falls off the bone. Remove the ribs from the braising liquid.

Tip: You can strain and reduce the braising liquid to use for a great sauce.

Stuffed Grape Leaves

This recipe is from *Lowfat Cooking For Dummies*. Grape leaves are easy to find bottled in most large markets. You can make these days ahead of time. They are served chilled. The small amount of lamb in the recipe is optional. Grind it in your food processor.

Tools: Large nonstick saucepan, large baking dish, ovenproof plate or heavy lid and foil

Yield: 20 to 30 stuffed leaves

4 cloves garlic, peeled and minced

2 teaspoons olive oil

2 ounces lean lamb, ground (optional)

1/2 cup finely chopped onion

1/4 cup finely chopped fennel

1/4 cup chopped fresh parsley

3/4 cup dry white or brown rice

Salt (optional)

1 tablespoon plus 1/3 cup fresh lemon juice

1 1/2 cups water

2 tablespoons raisins or currants

1/4 teaspoon ground nutmeg

20 to 30 grape leaves (if fresh, parboiled and dried, center stem removed if large and fibrous)

2 cloves garlic, peeled and slivered

1 Preheat the oven to 350°F.

2 In a small dish or bottle, combine the garlic and olive oil and set aside. In a large nonstick saucepan, heat the lamb (if desired), onion, fennel, and parsley for about 5 minutes, tossing, until the lamb is no longer pink. Drain any oil.

3 To the onion mixture, add the rice, salt (if desired), and 1 tablespoon lemon juice and heat until the rice is hot, about 2 minutes. Add the water, stir, cover, and cook for 20 minutes.

(continued)

4 Remove from the heat. Mix in the raisins (or currants) and nutmeg.

5 Place the leaves opened and flat on a board and drop about 1 table-spoon of the rice mixture onto each leaf. Wrap the leaves around the mixture, rolling and folding in the ends. Don't wrap tightly.

6 In a large baking dish lightly coated with no-stick vegetable oil spray, place the leaves wrapped side down and close to one another so that the wrapping stays neat.

7 Pour the olive oil and garlic over the leaves, weigh down with an oven-proof plate or foil and a heavy lid, and bake for 15 to 20 minutes.

8 Transfer to a serving dish, pour the remaining $^1/_3$ cup lemon juice and the slivered garlic cloves over the mixture, and chill, covered, for several hours.

Chips and Dips

Don't just rip open a bag of chips and put it on the table for a cocktail party. If you do, please don't tell people at the party that you bought this book!

Use your imagination when putting out chips, or delegate the task to someone else. Chips look great in a bowl; likewise for dips.

Any of these salsas from *Lowfat Cooking For Dummies* will be right at home at a Mexican-style fiesta or any party. You can use a blender or food processor or chop everything by hand. They're all great served with tortilla chips, bell pepper wedges, or celery sticks for dippers.

Salsa: Green for Go Cilantro

Tools: *Blender or food processor*

Yield: *About 2$^1/_2$ cups*

(continued)

¹/₂ cup chopped scallions, green part only

1 cup chopped cucumber

1 cup chopped mild Vidalia, Maui, or other sweet onion

¹/₂ cup chopped fresh cilantro

2 stalks celery

¹/₂ green bell pepper

1 tablespoon cider vinegar

2 tablespoons fresh lime juice

¹/₂ teaspoon sugar

Salt (optional)

3 yellow tomatoes

1 In a blender or food processor, place the scallions, cucumber, onion, cilantro, celery, green pepper, vinegar, lime juice, sugar, and salt to taste (if desired) and coarsely chop.

2 Add the tomatoes and coarsely shop.

Salsa: Moderately Spicy Yellow

Tools: *Blender or food processor*

Yield: *About 12 cups*

¹/₂ stalk celery

4 scallions, white part only

¹/₄ Spanish onion

2 large cloves garlic, peeled and minced

1 yellow bell pepper, cut in fourths

¹/₄ red bell pepper

3 large yellow tomatoes, or 3 cups yellow cherry tomatoes

1 4-ounce can chopped mild green chilies

¹/₄ cup fresh lime juice

1 tablespoon vinegar

¹/₂ teaspoon finely chopped jalapeno pepper

Salt (optional)

1 In a blender or food processor, place the celery, scallions, onion, garlic, and yellow and red pepper and coarsely chop.

2 Add the tomatoes, chilies, lime juice, vinegar, jalapeno, and salt to taste (if desired) and coarsely chop.

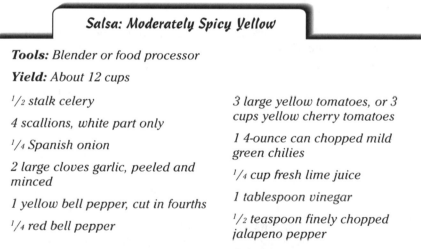

Salsa: Some Like It Red Hot

Hot and spicy salsa with a smoky base is especially satisfying. Surround the salsa with a few hot peppers to give guests a tip as to the heat. Make the dish ahead of time to incorporate the flavors. You can use a food processor or chop everything by hand.

Tools: *Blender or food processor*

Yield: *About 3 cups, or 12 ¹/₄-cup servings*

1 chipotle pepper, soaked for 30 minutes

1 small jalapeno pepper, with seeds, vein, and stem removed

1 red onion, peeled

¹/₄ cup chopped fresh cilantro (optional)

3 to 4 very ripe tomatoes

1 tablespoon cider vinegar

3 tablespoons fresh lime juice

¹/₂ teaspoon sugar

Salt (optional)

1 In a blender or food processor, place the chipotle and jalapeno and finely chop or nearly puree.

2 Add the onion and cilantro (if desired) and very coarsely chop.

3 Add the tomatoes, vinegar, lime juice, sugar, and salt to taste (if desired) and pulse just a few times.

Nuts

I'm a nut for nuts, but nuts, like chips, need some presentation effort. You can't just open a container of nuts and pour the contents into a bowl. You don't want any shells making their way onto your dance floor, so always get unshelled nuts. A surprisingly large number of people have severe allergies to nuts, so if you know that any of your guests have such allergies, don't even bother buying that particular kind of nut.

Scarborough Fair Toasted Herbed Nuts

Nuts   *Fresh herbs*

1 Mix together your favorite combination of nuts like Brazil nuts, hazelnuts (or filberts), pecans, walnuts, and peanuts and coat generously with fresh herbs (parsley, sage, rosemary, and/or thyme).

2 Bake in a 250°F oven for about twenty minutes before you plan to serve them.

Goes great with homemade beer and bathtub gin.

Seafood

Seafood is another hors d'oeuvre that screams "Cocktail party!" to your guests. And this is a broad category: Anything from sushi to shrimp can be used. The key is that the food be bite-sized. You don't want your guests trying to hold a conversation with a flounder in their hand!

While almost any kind of seafood can do, make sure that the seafood you serve is appropriate to your cocktail party and your crowd. Smelly fish will turn off your guests; salty fish will make them drink too much. Oysters are tricky. They're decadent but drippy, so if you serve them, guests will need napkins and tables.

The quintessential appetizer for the elegant soiree is the Shrimp Cocktail, given a flavorful kick in this recipe from *Lowfat Cooking For Dummies.*

Spiced Shrimp

Serve these shrimp cold or hot, with or without the shells, letting people peel their own and dip them in cocktail sauce or Spicy Dipping Sauce.

Tools: *2-quart saucepan*

Yield: *4 servings*

(continued)

12 ounces light beer, or 1 cup water

1 teaspoon dried basil, or 6 fresh basil leaves

¹/₂ to 1 teaspoon crushed red pepper (flakes) (optional)

¹/₂ teaspoon dried oregano

¹/₂ teaspoon dried thyme

¹/₄ teaspoon hot pepper sauce (optional)

¹/₂ teaspoon onion salt

2 tablespoons chili powder

12 ounces shrimp in the shell

1 In a 2-quart saucepan, place the beer or water, basil, red pepper (if desired), oregano, thyme, hot pepper sauce (if desired), onion salt, and chili powder. Whisk to combine.

2 Bring the mixture to a boil over medium-high heat. Add the shrimp.

3 Reduce the heat to medium, cover, and cook for 1 to 2 minutes or until the shrimp are opaque and bright pink. Remove from the heat and drain. If serving chilled, place the shrimp in an ice bath and drain again to both stop the cooking and chill quickly.

Spicy Dipping Sauce

¹/₂ cup ketchup

1 tablespoon grated horseradish (optional)

1 tablespoon brown sugar

¹/₂ teaspoon hot sauce

1 teaspoon prepared mustard

1 teaspoon soy sauce

In a small bowl, combine the ketchup, horseradish (if desired), brown sugar, hot pepper sauce, mustard, and soy sauce and mix well. Serve with the shrimp.

To spice shrimp only lightly, add 1 tablespoon Old Bay Seasoning to 1 inch white wine or beer. Steam the shrimp for 3 minutes or until opaque and bright pink.

This makes a great-looking treat for a table centerpiece or a buffet that works especially well at Christmas, when you can make it look like a Christmas tree.

The Shrimp Tree

60 cooked, peeled, headless shrimp

grapefruit

fancy lettuce

big bowl of favorite dipping sauce

candy canes or cranberry garlands

1 Put one of each shrimp on a sate stick (available at most Chinese stores), leaving a bit of room at the blunt end for your guests to hold them by.

2 Cut a grapefruit in half and place face down on a plate covered in fancy lettuce. Stick the sate sticks into the grapefruit half in a circular pattern moving towards the top center. The size and shape of the tree is determined by the size of the fruit, the amount of shrimp sticks you have, and how far you push the sticks in.

3 Place a big bowl of your favorite dipping sauce next to the tree. For a really festive treat, decorate the tree with little candy canes or cranberry garlands.

Raw Oysters on the Half Shell with a Champagne Mignonette

Nothing is more impressive and gutsy than consuming raw oysters on the half shell. People take turns "downing" these slimy delicacies and watch in awe as their turn approaches. Serving oysters with a champagne mignonette is a classic and flavorful method of preparation. From *Gourmet Cooking For Dummies*.

Yield: *8 oysters*

8 fresh oysters, shucked and kept in their liquid, shells rinsed

¹/₄ cup champagne

2 tablespoons champagne vinegar

8 drops lemon juice

1 tablespoon minced shallots

1 Place one oyster on each of 8 half shells and refrigerate until needed.

2 In a small bowl, mix together the champagne, vinegar, lemon juice, and shallots.

3 Pour some of the mixture over the oysters just prior to serving.

Smoked Salmon Beggars Purse with Creme Fraiche

Smoked salmon wrapped in a crepe is an impressive and simple flavor combination. These can be easily picked up and popped in your guests' mouths in one shot. From *Gourmet Cooking For Dummies*.

Specialty Tools: *5-inch crepe pan*

Yield: *8 Beggars Purses*

³/₄ cup milk	*1 teaspoon baking powder*
1 egg, lightly beaten	*vegetable oil as needed*
1 tablespoon butter, melted	*1 cup chopped smoked salmon*
1 cup flour	*2 tablespoons chopped chives*
1 tablespoon sugar	*8 teaspoons creme fraiche*
¹/₂ teaspoon baking soda	*8 long chives, blanched*

1 In a medium bowl, whisk the milk, egg, and butter together. Add the flour, sugar, baking soda, and powder and whisk together until smooth.

2 Brush the hot crepe pan lightly with the vegetable oil and pour the batter into the pan 1¹/₂ ounces at a time, rolling the batter around to cover the entire pan. Cook over medium heat until lightly golden on each side. Remove from the pan and repeat the process until you have at least 8 pancakes. Trim the crepes into perfectly round circles.

3 Toss the smoked salmon with the chives.

4 Place 1 teaspoon of the creme fraiche in the center of each crepe. Add 2 tablespoons of the smoked salmon mixture. Carefully bundle up the crepe, creating a little purse. Tie with a chive and serve slightly chilled.

Vegetables

Here's a tip: Don't serve Brussels sprouts. If your guests don't eat them at home, they won't eat them at your cocktail party. And Brussels sprouts are really gross cold.

Beyond that, about anything goes with vegetables. Your best bet: Cutting vegetables up into unique but manageable shapes and serving them with a nice dip. Just beware of double-dippers!

Six Dip Crudite

carrots	*red and green bell peppers*
broccoli	*mushroom rutabagas*
cauliflower	*green and yellow zucchini*

1 Make a basket or tray covered in the above veggies, cut into spears.

2 In six serving bowls, divide up a large jar of mayonnaise equally and then flavor each bowl with a different condiment like mango chutney, hot green curry paste, cyan and honey, garlic and lemon, or sesame oil and sesame seeds. Try a few of your own combinations, too.

If you're throwing a spy theme party, serve broccoli. The reason: The producer of almost all of the Bond films was Albert Broccoli, one of whose ancestors supposedly invented broccoli. See how many of your guests pick up on the broccoli-Bond connection!

If dippin' sticks bore you to tears, there are many more things you can make without resorting to cocktail wieners.

Salvidor Dali Olives

a few jars of pimento-stuffed Queen Mansanilla Olives

cream cheese

crushed walnuts

1 Drain the olives and pat dry.

2 Using your hands, encase the olive with cream cheese and form a smooth ball.

3 Roll in crushed walnuts and refrigerate till ready to serve. When cut in half, you get an eyeball with a green iris and a red pupil. Looks great on a plate with a happy face.

Garlic-Grilled Mushrooms

Tools: *Chef's knife, small bowl, brush for basting*

Preparation time: *about 10 minutes, plus time to preheat grill*

Grilling time: *About 5 minutes*

1 pound (500 g) mushrooms with large caps (portobello or shiitake)

¹/₃ cup (85 ml) extra-virgin olive oil

3 tablespoons (45 ml) lemon juice (preferably freshly squeezed), about 1 large lemon

2 teaspoons (10 ml) peeled and minced garlic, about 2 large cloves

salt and freshly ground pepper to taste

2 tablespoon (30 ml) minced fresh parsley (optional)

1 Preheat a charcoal fire or gas grill.

2 Clean the mushrooms with a damp paper towel. Remove the stems.

3 In a small bowl, combine the oil, lemon juice, and garlic. Brush the caps with the flavored oil and season with salt and pepper.

4 Place the caps on the grill, top side down, and grill for about 3 minutes. (Do not let them burn.) Turn the caps over and grill for another 2 to 3 minutes or until you can easily pierce the caps with a knife and the mushrooms are nicely browned.

5 Remove the mushrooms to a platter. Garnish with parsley and serve with toothpicks.

Source: *Cooking For Dummies*

Roasted Garlic Puree

Roasted garlic puree cries out to be spread on a piece of sourdough bread and makes a great vampire chaser. From *Gourmet Cooking For Dummies.*

Yield: *About ³/₄ cup*

4 bulbs garlic, tops cut off

3 cups milk

¹/₂ cup olive oil

salt and pepper

1 Place the garlic in a small saucepan, cover with the milk, and simmer for 10 minutes.

(continued)

2 Drain the milk and place the garlic bulbs bottom side down in an ovenproof pan. Add the olive oil and cover. Bake at 350°F for 1¹/₂ hours or until the bulbs are soft.

3 Cool, squeeze the soft garlic out of the skins, place in a blender with the olive oil it baked in, and puree until smooth.

Non-Traditional Fare

I have some non-traditional party theme ideas in Part II, so including a few unusual recipes seems only fair.

Soup Tubes

favorite chilled soup   *two-ounce test tubes*

1 Take your favorite chilled soup like a cold beef consomme or a creamy Mulligatawny (chilled curry soup) and serve them in two-ounce test tubes that you can get at your local hobby or science store.

2 Be sure to fill the test tube with a funnel to keep the sides clean. Don't forget to get a cute wooden rack to hold them upright on the table.

3 If the occasion calls for it, you may want to sparkle up your soup with a shot of vodka.

Cubed Eggs

1 To make this most delightful version of a hard-boiled egg, you need to acquire a handy little housewares tool known as an egg press.

2 Hard boil and peel the eggs and place in the egg press to cause the whites to get flat sided.

3 With mixtures of root-based food colors, paint the egg cubes either one color a side, or mix them up and make them look like an unsolved cube.

Desserts

Desserts go well with the sweet concoctions that are considered staples at cocktail parties. With so many dessert recipes out there, where do you start? Try this one. And if this doesn't work, try the other recipes in *Desserts For Dummies.*

Candied Orange Slices

Tools: *2 medium pots, slotted spoon*

Preparation time: *30 minutes*

Cooking time: *2 hours*

Yield: *1 cup (8 ounces)*

4 navel oranges or 6 lemons, sliced widthwise into ¹/₈-inch pieces.

3 cups (24 ounces) water

2¹/₂ cups (15 ounces) sugar

1 Bring a pot of water to a boil and drop in all the orange slices for about 30 seconds. Remove the slices with a slotted spoon and set aside for 3 minutes. Repeat the process with the same slices two more times, changing the water and bringing fresh water to a boil each time. This *blanching,* as it is called, removes the bitter acids from the peel.

2 In another pot, combine the water with 2 cups (12 ounces) sugar. After the mixture begins to boil, lower the heat to simmer. Drop the orange slices in and simmer uncovered for 2 hours. Add more water as it evaporates.

3 Drain the orange slices into a bowl and let the slices cool. Discard cooking liquid.

4 Dredge the orange slices in ¹/₂ cup (2 ounces) sugar and set on a platter for about 45 minutes to an hour. (*Dredging* means to drag through something, like flour or sugar, to coat lightly.)

How Much Food Do I Need?

Remember, starving guests aren't happy guests. But by definition, a cocktail party isn't a dinner party. The amount of food you require depends on the time of day and the length of your cocktail party.

Table 9-1 gives you an idea of how much food you need when serving guests for a two- to three-hour party in the early evening.

Table 9-1	Food — How Much for How Many		
	12 Servings	*24 Servings*	*48 servings*
Canapés	100	200	400
Dips, spreads, pates	1½ cups	3 cups	5 cups
Nuts	¾ cup	1½ lbs	3 lbs
Potato chips	2 (6-oz.) pkgs.	4 (6-oz.) pkgs.	8 (6-oz.) pkgs.
Corn chips	2 (9¼-oz.) pkgs.	4 (9¼-oz.) pkgs.	8 (9¼-oz.) pkgs.
Crackers	½ lb	1 lb	2 lbs
Bread rounds	2 (8-oz.) pkgs.	4 (8-oz.) pkgs.	8 (8-oz.) pkgs.

Afternoon parties will need about the same amount of food. Late-night parties, however, probably need less, because people will be coming from dinner to your party.

How Should I Present the Hors d'Oeuvres?

The art of presenting the hors d'oeuvres is the art of visual presentation. Nothing is more attractive to a lover of tasty tidbits than a beautiful morsel carefully skewered or framed in a delicate little pastry. Some people have presentation down and some people don't. If you don't, find a friend who does, or work in conjunction with your art director or party consultant.

The timing

Very few serving rules for hors d'oeuvres exist, but here are some guidelines:

✔ Usually you will send out a couple of different treats at once, but you needn't go overboard. If you have several snacks planned, stretch them out through the evening to surprise your guests.

✔ Begin serving approximately half an hour after the party has begun. You want to make sure that all of your guests have arrived so everyone can appreciate the extra effort you've made.

✔ Likewise, stop serving food about half an hour before the cocktail party ends. If your event is longer than two hours, you may run out much earlier, but that's all right. People aren't expecting a meal, and after a couple of hours they should be too busy dancing or conversing to notice that the serving has stopped.

✔ The intervals between serving can be decided by the length of your party. I recommend no more than ten minutes. Any less and you've lost the anticipation factor; much more and your guests will be salivating!

The serving staff

Having someone serve hors d'oeuvres to your guests is the classiest way to go. Even at a party with a not-so-elegant theme, such as Americana Backyard Barbecue, a serving staff adds a touch of class, even if you only have one waiter or waitress.

You should make certain that you have an adequate number of servers for your guests. A good guideline is that you should have one waiter or waitress for every 20–30 guests.

Another key consideration for your serving staff is the path you want them to take. Here are a few guidelines:

✔ Arrange the servers' path to maximize the number of guests they get exposure to.

✔ Alter the path. Send a server out one way the first time, a different way the next. This not only gives guests who may have been missed the first time a prime opportunity for a tasty treat the second time, but it allows your server to avoid the party glutton.

✔ Troubleshoot the path. You don't want a waiter tripping over a loose power cord and spilling your elegant hors d'oeuvres all over a guest!

Because you will likely have a few vegetarians at your cocktail party, when you send your servers out you should always keep vegetarian hors d'oeuvres on a separate tray or at least on one part of the tray.

The table

Although I usually recommend having your snacks served, certain theme parties beg for the food to be displayed on a table. If you go this route, either you or the caterer has to make the table look special. In addition to tablecloths, I've seen the following at cocktail parties:

- Sheets or tacky '60s or '70s curtains
- Wrapping paper
- Astroturf
- Palm leaves
- Toy soldiers, for a cocktail party on Remembrance Day (Canada's version of what the U.S. calls Memorial Day)

Friar Tuck, eat your heart out!

I once threw a cocktail party where a very long table was covered with tin foil. Pickles, vegetables, fruit, crackers, and various tiny breads were piled high on the table. It looked like a feast fit for a king, but there wasn't anything that required a plate. It required very little maintenance and no servers. The caterer prepared the table just before the party began, so everything was fresh. He set up and left immediately.

Although this method of serving was cost effective, at the end of the evening I had a table that was still covered with food, and no jars or Tupperware to put it in. (I should point out that although everything was tasty, there was no way in the world that my guests could consume it all. It was piled so high it was comical.) I ended up tossing it all into a large garbage can. What a waste!

Dali does hors d'oeuvres

You can get creative with your hors d'oeuvres, too. I remember a Surrealist cocktail party in San Francisco. Helium balloons were up on the twelve-foot ceiling and on the end of each string coming down was tied a tasty shrimp. You didn't even have to use your hands.

Picking a Caterer

Before choosing a caterer, you need to decide on your theme and have an idea of how many people will attend. Base your catering budget on these things. Other considerations include:

- ✔ Will the caterer also supply the serving staff?
- ✔ If the snacks are set up on a buffet table, do they decorate the area? Some caterers specialize in extra decorative touches, but don't assume that.
- ✔ Do they specialize in the type of food you desire?
- ✔ Do they deliver the treats and leave, or do they stay for the evening and clean up?

In many cases you will be able to either make the snacks yourself or have a friend who is great in the kitchen give you a hand, but if your ideas are challenging and you can afford a caterer, here are some suggestions on how to find one:

- ✔ **The Yellow Pages.** If you are going to go this route, you should call several companies and compare prices. You should also pay attention to the way they speak to you. If they sound impatient or impolite, you're off to a bad start. If you have time, you should meet them in person.
- ✔ **Ask your friends.** Chances are that you know someone who has hired a caterer or been to an event where hors d'oeuvres were served.
- ✔ **Ask the manager or owner of your favorite restaurant.** If he doesn't jump up and offer his services first, he will at least know of some caterers with solid reputations.

Repeat business with a twist

JAYMZ SAYZ

I have a favorite Japanese restaurant that had never catered an event before. I wanted to have a Sunset Sushi cocktail party on the roof of the studio I was recording in. Luckily the studio was only a block from the restaurant. The manager went out of his way to make sure that this catering job would not be his last.

The waiters set up tables and decorated them with Japanese lanterns and rice paper. They even set up a little hut using bamboo poles and leaves. Not only was the food delicious, but the price was right! This proves that sometimes giving the job to someone who appreciates your regular business is better than hiring someone that you've never met from an advertisement or phone book.

Part V
Doing the Party Thing

The 5th Wave   By Rich Tennant

"Careful Janis - it's the clown. He's heading toward the seltzer bottle again."

In this part...

*P*anicked because the party is only a week
away and you don't know what you should
be doing? Afraid that something will go wrong
and that you won't know what to do? Relax. You
have a lot to do, and something will go wrong.
Stop that — you're supposed to be relaxing! This
part contains a chapter with my handy-dandy
little party-planning checklist of what to do when
and a chapter on troubleshooting. Read the
chapters, learn from them, and greet your guests
with confidence.

Chapter 10

Countdown to the Party

. . . .

In This Chapter

▶ Duties of the host/hostess

▶ What to look for in a bartender

▶ What to look for in a waiter or waitress

▶ The party checklist

. . . .

I've been to several parties over the years where something was forgotten. Like the record release party where the host spent so much time on the hors d'oeuvres display that he forgot to clean the bathrooms. When several female guests complained, he had no one else to turn to — so he ended up cleaning the bathroom himself, leaving him flustered for the entire evening. Or the party host whose invitations didn't include a contact number, only the name of the restaurant, so frustrated guests called the restaurant for information — only to be referred to a bartender who knew nothing about the party and could have cared less.

When planning your party, you want to make sure that you have everything checked, with time to spare. With that in mind, this chapter gives you tips on hiring the right staff for your party and a timetable of things to check.

Finalizing Your Staff

Just as planning a party is easier with more people (see Chapter 1), putting on the party becomes a little more enjoyable with a few helping hands. Before the party begins, the host can be involved with anything. But after the guests start arriving, the host needs to just be a congenial host.

What kind of help you need depends on what type of party you're throwing. Let me add that I'm not talking about musicians or DJs here; you can find out more about those in Chapter 7. What I mean by party help is a bartender, a waiter or waitress, perhaps even a greeter. You may also need someone to check coats and help clean up, but those are less-involved tasks. Obviously, if you're throwing a small party at home, you can handle most, if not all, of those tasks, but if you're planning a bigger party, staffing is critical to the success of your party.

Once you've thrown several parties, you'll have a network of people that you can hire or that can give you good references for good workers. What do you do until then? Follow some of the tips in the following sections.

The party host/hostess

For parties at home or at small venues, the party host is the person who is at the door greeting each and every guest, and his or her name should be on the invitation (no matter how many people are working together on the party). The various other tasks should be delegated as much as possible; nothing is worse than the host flying around all stressed out at the party. Obviously, if you're only throwing a party for ten people, you're probably doing a solo act.

For larger parties, you need to separate the greeting and host functions — especially if you don't feel comfortable greeting the guests. In such cases, you need to appoint an official door greeter. Look for a person who does the following:

- ✔ Greets people with a smile
- ✔ Takes coats or boots
- ✔ Shows ladies where they can freshen up before making their entrance
- ✔ Points out the host or hostess, especially at large parties where strangers are invited
- ✔ Explains the lay of the land — where to find the bar, where to find hors d'oeuvres, and any other pertinent information

The actual host of the party can do this job, but if someone else is available who can readily handle the responsibility, then the host can be the second person to greet the guest. He then shows guests around the party, offers them hors d'oeuvres, gets a drink in their hand, and leads guests into the nearest conversational group.

When introducing people of varied ages, proper etiquette dictates that you introduce the younger person to the older one. Men are always presented to ladies, regardless of age difference. Try to introduce new guests to more than one other person. Do introductions slowly, giving people a chance to remember the new names, and offer a very brief biographical overview that may help start conversation. If you know of anything the guests have in common, mention it.

After you've greeted everybody at the door and the party is in full swing, make the rounds and try to get a couple of words in with every guest in attendance. If you notice someone who seems a little out of place, try to make her feel welcome and introduce her to others that she may be able to strike up a conversation with. Grabbing a single guest and interrupting a group of people in conversation to make a new introduction is not at all out of character for a host. And keep people circulating. Watch out for developing cliques of people. Try and mix them up with new guests. You want to do so discreetly, but it's considered normal etiquette for the host.

The bartender

To the person who knows nothing about it, bartending may seem like a simple job. But like any professional job, it requires careful study to become an expert. I'm not talking so much about the mixing of the drinks themselves — a matter in itself — I'm talking about waiting on customers.

What do you look for in a bartender? Try the following:

- ✔ **Good appearance.** In addition to being neat, a bartender needs to be alert, attentive, bright, cheerful, courteous, and easy-going.

- ✔ **Good listening skills.** Bartenders should be good listeners but not take sides or play favorites between guests.

- ✔ **Sobriety.** Bartenders should not drink with guests while on the job.

Believe it or not, I once had to fire a bartender at a New Year's Eve party for being drunk. He arrived staggering, and had to ask three times for a corkscrew. I answered twice; the third time I asked him to leave. The other bartender had to work twice as hard, and I had to help out.

✔ **Professionalism.** Bartenders should be prompt. If they're supplying equipment, they should not only have the equipment with them when they arrive, but they should also arrive early enough to set up the bar. Quiz them on a few of the equipment terms in Chapter 8 to make sure that they know their stuff. And check to see what the bartenders expect to do after the party; while they aren't expected to wash glasses, they are expected to leave the bar clean and neat.

✔ **Good references.** If you're hiring a bartender for the first time, check out some previous employers to see if he met their party needs.

One other trait to look for in a bartender: discernment. As the host, you are responsible for your guests, even the ones who go away drunk. You want a bartender who knows when to say when, so to speak. Most professional bartenders will not serve a drunk person, but be careful about the attitude of a non-professional bartender who's one of the gang. He may be inclined to pour them strong.

Also, the bartender's job is not to force a drink on someone who would rather not partake. In this era of so many people wanting to remain clean and sober, the last thing you want is for a bartender to push alcohol on someone who's trying to kick the habit.

You, the host, are responsible for providing the alcohol, and making sure that you have the proper ingredients if you're going to offer any special drinks. Make sure that you have your mocktail and smartini options (see Chapter 8) and that the bartender is well aware of them.

The waiting staff

Like bartending, waiting on guests at a party seems like an easy job. But waiters and waitresses mingle with the crowd; while doing so, their attitude can rub off on the guests. So look for waiters and waitresses who can handle the workload with enthusiasm, or at least a professional air.

Other things to look for in waiters or waitresses include the following:

✔ **Good appearance.** If they have to dress for the theme, make sure that they feel comfortable in the required outfit.

✔ **Good balance.** Walking with a tray full of martinis is almost like a circus trapeze act. You don't want your guests to get wet or dirty, and you don't want to waste valuable alcohol or food.

✔ **Professionalism.** Waiters and waitresses should arrive early enough to receive instructions. And they should be able to understand their role at your party without feeling like a slave.

Remember that you are the one in charge of keeping hors d'oeuvres circulating through the crowd. You may have to tell a waiter, "Quick — take this out NOW!" At those times, you don't want a waiter who acts like a disgruntled postal worker, so look for a waiter with a good attitude.

✔ **Good references.** Unlike with a bartender, you can take a chance on someone who hasn't waited a great deal, as long as she meets the other criteria.

When you're in a club or restaurant and you meet a waiter or waitress whose work you admire, try to steal him or her for one day. Usually you can, if you give the waiter enough notice. Waiters and waitresses prefer doing private parties. They know how much money they're getting, they're meeting new people, and they're in a new scene.

Be careful hiring friends

While hiring friends may be the easy way to staff your party, think before you call. Most friends won't want to clean up or do menial tasks. Some will find it beneath them to come to your party and actually work. If you pay someone else a fee — even if it's only an honorarium of $50 — then you have the right to tell that person that you're not going to pay him if he doesn't do a good job. You're allowed to tell someone off or deduct wages; but if that someone is a friend, he may get angry, and you could wreck your friendship.

Other staff members to consider

Large parties may require additional help, including

✔ **Consultants.** This book gives you all of the details you need to throw most parties, but you may run into situations — the end-all affair for a couple of thousand — where you'd feel more comfortable hiring someone to share the credit or the blame.

✔ **Dance instigators.** If your party involves dancing, don't just wait for the first brave couple to break the ice. Hire a few couples who love to dance to come to the party with the understanding that they will brave the stares of others to start the conga line.

If you can't think of friends who will do this, contact any dance studio to see if they have a few students willing to make an appearance at your party for an invitation and a free limo ride. With ballroom dancing enjoying a major resurgence, you'd be surprised at how willing couples are to strut their stuff across an actual dance floor — not just their classroom.

✔ **Cleanup crew.** In addition to having someone to wash the glasses at the end of the night (even rental places expect glassware to be returned clean), have someone around when the party starts. It doesn't look good if the host of the party is running around with a vacuum cleaner because someone spilled an ashtray.

Unless you have an unlimited budget and a great insurance policy, don't hire a valet for your party. Any dents and dings they put in cars will put dents and dings in your wallet.

The Party Countdown Checklist

Advance planning is the key to a successful cocktail party. With that in mind, I offer my party countdown checklist. Any expert on human behavior will tell you that making a checklist is the best way to get things done, and it's a good way to stay organized so that you are better prepared to deal with that inevitable last-minute crisis.

Some of these guidelines will not apply for smaller parties, and if what you're doing is simple, then you can simply start two weeks before the party.

Four to six weeks before

You've probably just made up your mind that you're definitely going to have the party. Here's what you need to do now:

- ✔ Decide on the size of party that you're going to have. (See Chapter 1.)

- ✔ Decide on the theme of your party. (See Chapters 3 and 4 for ideas.)

- ✔ Decide where you are going to have the party. (See Chapter 2.) If it's at your home, and the party room needs work, now is the time to get on it. If you're renting a venue, confirm with them and make any necessary deposits.

- ✔ Make up your preliminary guest list.

- ✔ Create your invitations.

- ✔ If you're booking live entertainment or a disc jockey, find out who you want and contact them.

- ✔ If you're hiring extra help, such as bartenders or caterers, confirm with them now.

Three weeks before

Now that you've got the place and the kind of party set, you need to focus on more specific details:

- ✔ Address and mail your invitations.

- ✔ Plan your drinks and food menu (stay with your theme).

- ✔ Plan the look and ambiance and make a "needed supplies" list. Figure out any items that you'll have to rent or buy. Start making the other items.

- ✔ Think about customizing cocktail napkins; make arrangements with a printer to get yours done.

- ✔ Reserve any barware, glassware, linen, tablecloths, equipment, and/or furniture that you'll need to rent.

One week before

You'll find plenty of reasons to get stressed on the day of your party, so take care of anything that you can early. You want to be able to relax at your party. A week before your party, make a shopping list and start getting everything you need. You've already decided what hors d'oeuvres and drinks you're going to make; go through the recipes and make a shopping list.

✔ Buy liquor and mixers (see Chapter 8 for tips on estimating the amount needed). Have extra liquor on hand, but also have the hours and number of the nearest liquor store handy on the day of the party.

In a BYOB situation, people invariably bring booze but no mixer. Even people who don't drink rarely bring their own orange juice or soda. You don't want to run out of mixer or juice, so buy extra.

✔ Also buy any nonperishable staples from your shopping list: olives, flour, sugar, anchovies, and so on.

✔ Double-check on any barware that you are borrowing or renting, and make sure that you have the right glassware and swizzle sticks coming.

✔ Check to see that you have the necessary tables. Do you want to rent one or two? If so, make the arrangements now. And check to see if the tables can be delivered or if they will fit in your car.

✔ Check to see that you have enough doilies and tablecloths.

✔ Check to see if you have enough ashtrays. (Of course, you've already thought about where people will smoke, haven't you? If not, see Chapter 6.)

✔ Finalize your music plans. Do you need any equipment? If you're making a tape, use a high-quality cassette, and don't leave it until the last minute.

✔ Get toothpicks, the ones for cocktail olives and hors d'oeuvres.

✔ Order flowers.

Four days before

By this point, you should complete planning everything that you can. Do it now; try to avoid leaving details to the last minute.

✔ Polish silver, brass, and copper and wrap it in plastic sheeting.

✔ Check on guests who haven't given an R.S.V.P.

If you haven't heard from someone, a quick phone call that says "I haven't heard from you yet. I hope to see you; there are some people I really want you to meet" will suffice.

✔ Work out the furniture layout in your mind or on paper.

> ✔ Check your party clothes and see if anything needs to be washed or dry cleaned.

Two days before

You're probably tempted to do these things the day of the party, but don't wait.

> ✔ If the party is at your house, decorate your party room and then vacuum and dust.

> ✔ If the party is at a venue, try to drop by and take another look to make sure that no unwanted "surprises" — such as paint or construction — are taking place.

> ✔ If decorating a rental venue, then do any prepping of materials that you can.

> ✔ Create freezer space for extra ice.

> ✔ Buy your fresh food and ice.

> ✔ Prepare hors d'oeuvres and party dishes that can be frozen.

One day before

You're probably starting to get butterflies about your party now. Don't forget to do the following:

> ✔ Lay out your party clothes.

> ✔ Pick up any rental items you need.

> ✔ If you're hosting the party at your home, arrange for a space for coats and boots or umbrellas.

> ✔ If you're renting a space, then organize things together in bags or boxes and label them so you're not digging around frantically at the venue.

> ✔ Don't put off until tomorrow what you can do today. Finish anything that you possibly can.

The day of the party

Your goal, other than to have a great party, is to get in one hour of your own time — a quick nap, a shower — before your party. I always hope for it, and it rarely happens, but don't give up trying.

Before you go for that hour of your own, however, you need to do a few more things:

- ✔ Remove frozen foods for defrosting.
- ✔ Prepare the food as early in the day as possible.
- ✔ If the party's not at home, go to the venue and put up your decorations right after preparing the food.
- ✔ Set up the bar — have liquor, mixers, and beer cooling; cut and prepare the garnishes; and pick up equipment.
- ✔ Test your audio system and lighting. You can always send someone out for batteries or a light bulb before the party begins.
- ✔ Put out your flowers.
- ✔ Freshen up your bathroom by placing clean towels, fresh soap, and tissues out, and make sure that nothing is in there that you don't want someone to see.
- ✔ Walk through your party area with trouble in mind. Do you see a lamp or vase that's just waiting to get knocked over? Fix it now.
- ✔ Have your hair done and get your nails manicured.

A half-hour before start time

Invariably, everything is not absolutely perfect. You strive, you hope, and you pray, but something will not be quite as you dreamed. Unfortunately, the flawless party only happens in the movies. It doesn't matter. The guests are about to arrive. Your job is to pretend that everything is perfect. Your guests will never know the difference. When you greet people, you're expected to be in a good mood, because you'll be setting the tone for the whole evening. Your greeting says, "Everything is fine. Come on in. Welcome. Have a good time."

So a half-hour before the guests arrive, do whatever you have to do to feel good. If you've been laboring long and hard on something that just is not working, abandon it. It's not worth it. Go lie down for ten minutes. Or make yourself a drink. Or freshen up. Do whatever it is that you do in order to feel good.

If you haven't showered and dressed, well, don't wait. Do it now. You're expected to look as good or better than the guests. Remember, you wanted to host a party because it would be fun.

Do you feel better now? Get up. I hear footsteps. Here they come. Okay, now, smile!

Chapter 11

Mishaps and Misfits: How to Handle Them

* *

In This Chapter

▶ Bad weather and cancellations

▶ Accidents and spills

▶ Party crashers: The good, the bad, and the ugly

▶ How to get people to leave your fabulous party

* *

*M*ost of the time you don't want to be the focal point of your cocktail party. But circumstances arise when that's inevitable — especially when there's a problem.

This chapter looks at the most common problems and offers suggestions on how to deal with them. You can't avoid troubles, but you can handle them smoothly and quickly.

Bad Weather

You really have no control over this variable. If the weather is just mildly bad, it may actually help the attendance of an indoor party. But if weather is downright horrendous or dangerous, you can't really do much but enjoy the attendance of a few hardy friends, eat all the hors d'oeuvres and call it dinner. Save the liquor, of course, for the next party.

If you're planning an outdoor party, then you really should have a contingency plan and state "Rain or Shine" on the invitation. In geographic areas that are subject to power outages, have a good supply of festive candles and matches and your guests won't even realize that it wasn't part of the planned fun.

The Party is Postponed or Canceled

Regardless of your planning and hard work, sometimes something occurs that means you have no choice; you have to cancel or postpone the party. What do you do?

Go through your grief process quickly. Shock, denial, anger — get to acceptance quickly and get on with it. Cancel the party with class and your guests will understand. Get out your guest list and your pen, and do the following:

✔ If the party is truly off, then move quickly to let your guests know. If the party is formal, and you still have plenty of time, then write, following the style of the original invitation. If you're getting close to the wire, then use the phone, fax, or e-mail.

✔ If the party is canceled without a make-up date, then you need to give a brief explanation as to why. If you've come up with a make-up date (and make sure that the date is solid), then you aren't required to give an explanation for the change.

✔ If you're postponing the party to a later date, then you are required to reinvite all of the original guests. If you need to add a few more, do so, but don't leave anyone out who was on the original list.

The Venue Manager or Owner is Difficult

If this is the first party you've done at a particular location, you may discover things while actually setting up that weren't clear when you were just talking about it. You may even discover on the day of your party that you never want to have another party at this location again. Don't do anything until after the party is over.

At all costs, avoid getting into a big confrontation with the venue managers over something or other on the day of the party. They have all the leverage — you need the venue. You may have to grit your teeth and play the game, but this approach is best *until your guests have left.* After you've done a few parties, you'll get a handle on it, and after your parties are successful, you will have some leverage of your own.

Your Guests Arrive Before You're Ready

If your guests arrive before the scheduled time on the invitation, then they should be embarrassed, not you. If you're not ready at the start time, then that's your problem as the host. But either way, give them a drink and get them situated somewhere out of your way where they can hang out for a few minutes until you're ready.

Accidents and Spills

For large parties, you have to have a couple of troubleshooters and people that are picking up after the guests. If an accident happens, you have to make the guests feel like it wasn't their fault that they broke a glass or put their face in a cake. Put that smile on your face and say that it doesn't matter. Remember the mood of the cocktail party, and don't let any stress of the host interfere with the tinkling of ice and the pleasant chatter and laughter.

Do everything you can to make guests feel good after they feel stupid.

Drunken Guests

There are times when money laid down at a bar should not be accepted, no matter the status of the person or how difficult refusing a drink may be. If a drunk is getting obnoxious, remember the technique that was perfected by the legendary 21 Club speakeasy: Have a friend act equally "drunk" for the sake of calming the guest down.

Under no circumstances do you want a drunken guest to wander out of your party with the intention of driving off to another place or home. Get a few friends involved, and discreetly sneak the guest's keys away from him. Make arrangements for a friend to drive him home or for him to take a cab. If the drunk insists that he wants to drive, then his keys will just have to mysteriously turn up "lost."

Responsible drinking is one of the most crucial areas of *your* responsibility as host, and sometimes one of the hardest, but don't put your guests' or other innocent people's lives at risk.

Party Crashers

You probably won't have a problem with uninvited people showing up at your first parties. But when you begin to throw parties at venues, you increase your chances of having someone try to crash your party.

Not all party crashers are bad; some are good. Sometimes you want these people and you feel dumb that you didn't invite them. Even if you don't know them, they might look fabulous and have the right smile and the right energy. They might show up at the door saying "I'm not on the list, but you really need me at your party." Well, sometimes you really do if your party could use some livening up.

But bankers and drag queens do not always mix. Occasionally, someone will show up at the door that you know you don't want inside. Never make it sound like you don't want the person to come in. Doing so can lead to a physical confrontation.

One way to screen out people right at the door is to tell them that the cover charge is $25 instead of whatever it is. Inflate the price to a cover that no sane person would pay. And then add, "I don't know why anyone would want to pay that."

Other times, you can misrepresent the party. Tell the unwanted guest that the party is being held for the Save the Geoduck Foundation. "Hey, man. These people are weird." You don't want to tell him no, so tell him how geeky or expensive it is instead.

In a situation where you're in a questionable part of town, you may want to hire a security guy from a club in the area. Never hire goons that use physical confrontation. You will find that the clubs that have the most problems with bathrooms getting trashed and such are the ones that have the most intimidating door presence. Bars that have hard-core security staff also have a great deal more vandalism, because it's the one way people can get back at the bar.

Kicking Someone Out of Your Party

If you find yourself in a situation of having to kick someone out, never sound like you're the one who wants them out of there. I recommend some variation of what the 21 Club perfected — have your "drunk" bond with the unwanted guest and wander them out and down the street.

If you or your door staff needs to try and get someone out, then I recommend that you say something like "Man, the boss has gotten some complaints about you. Now to me, you seem like the nicest guy in the world, but the boss wants you to leave. And if I don't ask you to trip on out of here then look, this is my job, man, and I don't make much money." You should be able to walk most monsters outside saying "Hey, come on back down tomorrow. We'll try it again."

Remember Mr. T's advice: "No Tough Guy Stuff." Even if you have big guys on the door, avoid a show of force that could lead to physical confrontation. As Mr. T used to say about being a doorman, you're the first person people see when they come in. You're supposed to set the tone. You're nice to everybody. Invite them in. Say, "Come on in. Have yourself a nice evening." Don't play the big tough guy at the door, because those people won't be your friends later. It'll be a big power trip and you don't want to have that after people start drinking.

End Your Party Well in Advance of Closing Hour

At the end of the night, bars can get a bit uptight about people leaving. If you're holding the party in a bar that's often harassed by the liquor authorities, you can find that they can get rather rude about making people leave. Remember, the club can be subjected to fines if people are still drinking or even holding containers with alcohol in them after a certain hour. So think ahead and get your friends out of there; do not put your friends or the club into violation of the law.

Guests Who Won't Leave

Cocktail etiquette dictates that people leave at the end time that's stated on your invitation. However, this is not always the case. If the guests show no signs of departing, discreetly ask a close friend to make a very conspicuous exit. Offering *final* nightcaps also works as a good hint.

Fifteen minutes after the end time:

- ✔ All hors d'oeuvres should be removed, if they haven't been already.
- ✔ The liquor should "run out."
- ✔ The music should stop.

Nothing clears 'em out quite like the proposal of home movies or slides, you know, a two-hour slide show of your last trip. Or some really loud, obnoxious music.

Keep a Record

If you intend to keep on giving parties, and you want them to continually improve and be different, then keep a record of your parties. A simple file or manila envelope filled with the overall stats will suffice, but do get down the following party stats for future reference:

- ✔ **The date, time, place, kind of party, and the reason for giving the party.**
- ✔ **The guests:** Who were they, and was it a successful party mix? Did people converse and have fun? Take notes the day after your party, and you'll be able to look back in the future and decide if you want to go with the same guests or alter the mix slightly.
- ✔ **The menu:** Did your snacks get swooped up? Did you get positive comments? Did you have enough for the amount of people? Whatever you do, you don't want to always have the same hors d'oeuvres so often that your parties become predictable and unexciting.
- ✔ **The drinks served:** What did they cost? Did you have enough? Were you getting requests for drinks you didn't have?
- ✔ **Decorations and ambiance.**
- ✔ **Special private notes:** This section is the one that you'll really want to remember. You know, those things like "Kevin ended up in the bathroom with Bill's wife" or "Never invite Tim and Cindy — they argued all night."
- ✔ **Total cost of the party:** Record any comments about good deals, any glassware that was broken, or a barman or barmaid that you particularly liked.

Part VI

The Part of Tens

In this part...

I won't lie to you: The chapters in this part are basically glorified lists. But they're fun lists, things like wonderful cocktail Web sites, great cocktail films, and cocktail heroes. Oh, and just for appearances, I threw something practical in here, too — answers to questions frequently posed by cocktail party guests. Enjoy!

Chapter 12
Ten Things Guests Should Know

*G*uests are almost as responsible for the success of a cocktail party as the host. The host can have a terrific theme, delightful decorations, and elegant hors d'oeuvres, but if the guests just sit around and wait to be entertained, the party will be a flop.

So what should you, as a cocktail party guest, keep in mind? This chapter gives you some do's and don'ts. Remember, after the host, the person most responsible for making sure that you have a good time is you.

Should a Guest be Fashionably Late?

No. Fashionable lateness is less fashionable than it used to be. Don't be early, either. Invariably, your host is running around with last-minute duties. Give him a couple extra minutes. Show up ten to fifteen minutes after the scheduled start time.

Should Guests Arrive Bearing Gifts?

Gifts are not in the cocktail party tradition. No flowers. No gift for the host. No bottle of wine. A cocktail party is not to be confused with a dinner party. The guests should just show up looking fabulous, ready to smile and be talkative.

If the Invitation Doesn't Specify, How Should Guests Dress?

A good cocktail party invitation (see Chapter 5) should always include any dress requirements or at least hint at the theme, but if that information is lacking, try calling the host to see what the dress code will be. If the invitation doesn't have a phone number or you can't contact the host, try someone else who you know is invited to the party. That way, if you guess wrong, at least you're not the only one! Or call the venue, and find out if they can offer any help.

If you are guessing, use the time of day and time of year as guides, and then dress better rather than worse. Parties in the afternoon tend to be more casual than parties at night. Parties in the summer tend to be less formal than parties in the fall and winter.

How Should Guests Interact?

When you are invited to a cocktail party, especially a small one, you've received a compliment. The host invited you because she thought you could add to the party! Now you have to live up to her expectations.

Learn to mingle

If you're a guest, and have always found yourself nervous about mingling, the time is right for you to change all that. Mingling is one thing you just have to *do* and it's one thing that is best that you do *alone*. If you want to meet new people at a party, you have a much better chance of going at it alone, as opposed to as a "couple" or with a friend. If you've never been good at mingling, and it's something you even dread, all I can say is you just have to dive in and go for it.

Remember that a cocktail party is all about meeting new people. If you spot someone you'd really like to meet, then this is the perfect place to just walk up to him, introduce yourself, and tell him that you've been wanting to meet him. Who can object to that? A little flattery will get you everywhere, and if you have a couple of questions ready beyond the introduction, the conversation will be off and running.

You may want to have a couple of stand-by topics in the back of your mind — a new movie or contemporary news item — to bring up if a conversation obviously needs changing.

Ask questions

Think about the talk show host, trying to initiate a conversation.

The simplest way to dive right in is to engage someone in a small-talk type conversation. "Mmm, did you try the shrimp?" or "Jaymz is a crazy guy, huh? Where do you know him from?" The key is to keep asking questions until you discover some mutual interests that keep the conversation rolling.

What Shouldn't a Guest Say When Ordering a Cocktail?

Remember, cocktail parties — even cocktail parties with crazy themes — are more sophisticated affairs than just tapping a keg of beer and inviting your friends over. As such, you don't want to commit a gaffe at the bar. Here are a few suggestions on things not to say when ordering a cocktail:

- ✔ "Make it on the rocks — and can I have some ice in that, too?"
- ✔ "May I have a vodka martini with two straws."
- ✔ "I'll have a straight Vermouth."
- ✔ "Is there a bologna-flavored vodka yet?"
- ✔ "I'll have one of those trendy drinks with the Italian name — a martino!"
- ✔ "Can I get it to go? I have got a long drive ahead of me."
- ✔ "What kind of beer do you have?"

Should a Guest Just Light Up a Cigar?

No. The smoking gentleman or lady should ask the host, "Mind if I smoke?" A cigar smoker may look on smoking as suave and refreshing, but because some people may have strong aversions to smoke — and they may be guests at your party — cocktail etiquette dictates that a person look around or ask before lighting up a big one. Courtesy is appreciated.

How Does a Guest Know It's Time to Go?

Remember, cocktail parties start and end on time. When the clock hits the end time included in your invitation, then graciously leave.

Beyond that, here are some signs from your host that it's time to go:

- ✔ Your host breaks out the punk rock albums.
- ✔ The host starts showing slides of his summer vacation.
- ✔ The host circulates in the room, explaining the concept of the "last call."
- ✔ The television gets turned on to the Weather Channel.
- ✔ The room lights come on.
- ✔ The host starts vacuuming.

Should a Guest Send a Thank-You?

Yes. Traditional cocktail etiquette dictates that the guest send a thank-you card or note to the host. The guest should at least leave a phone message the next day, but the host may have to be satisfied with a "Great party!" while saying goodbye.

If you're a host, and you find that you're not getting many thank you cards from your guests, don't despair! The very best thank you is an invitation to another party. If someone attends your party and doesn't send a thank-you, but invites you over, consider that thanks enough!

What Other "Don'ts" Should a Guest Observe?

- ✔ Don't bring anyone to the party who you can't trust or who might get out of hand.
- ✔ Don't pursue heated political debates with others who may have had a bit too much to drink. In the morning, you'll forget why whether the professor on *Gilligan's Island* was a conservative or a liberal was so important.

✔ Don't bring children. Children are wonderful, but cocktail parties are strictly for adults — and do you really want your children's lungs filling up with smoke from your cigar?

✔ Don't turn on the television for basketball scores. The only time anyone should even think about turning a television on at a cocktail party is at a TV-related theme or to show a Matt Helm or "Rat Pack" movie (see Chapter 14).

✔ Don't butt out your cigar in an empty glass.

✔ Don't request Michael Bolton at a karaoke party.

✔ And most important of all — DO NOT DRIVE if you've had lots of alcohol; make arrangements for a designated driver or call a cab.

Chapter 13

Ten Essential Cocktail Web Sites

The World Wide Web features thousands of topics on thousands of subjects, so experienced Web "surfers" won't be surprised to find the cocktail movement well represented. Want to get a taste of what's out there? This chapter has ten of my favorite cocktail Web sites.

The Web sites featured in this chapter were current as of the time of this writing, but even the best Web sites disappear and reappear with great fluidity, almost as if they're written in sand on a beach. Good Web Browser programs (like Yahoo! or AltaVista) should be able to pick out the cocktail party sites that are still active by using keywords to find them. Such keywords include:

- ✔ Cocktail
- ✔ Bachelor/Bachelorette
- ✔ Space Age Bachelor Pad Music
- ✔ Spy, Spy Jazz
- ✔ Latin Music: Cha Cha, Mambo, Tango, Rumba, Bossa Nova
- ✔ Lounge, Loungecore

Browsers can also usually find what you need by entering a cocktail music artist's name.

Need a primer on the Web?

What's the Web, you say? Sounds like you need a primer on the Internet. A couple of good how-to guides to get you up and "surfing" on the Internet are *The Internet For Dummies,* 4th edition, by John R. Levine, Carol Baroudi, and Margaret Levine Young and *The Internet For Macs For Dummies,* 2nd edition, by Charles Seiter (both published by IDG Books Worldwide, Inc.)

Many domains, like my site (http://www.wiredkingdom.com/beehive) give you direct links to other cocktail-related Web sites for others in the cocktail movement, like Combustible Edison, Juan Esquivel, or Jack Diamond.

The Blue Lizard Cocktail Club

Although this "club" takes over the lounges at the Waldorf Hotel in Vancouver, British Columbia, Canada, on the third Saturday of every month, this Web site offers "a world where Happy Hour is perpetual." Dig it?

http://www.webpool.com/bluelizard/

Club Montepulciano (London, UK)

In addition to lots of information about the club and the London scene, this site — at least, at the time of this writing — features something called "Eleanor's Vegetable Tips," a truly unique way to present veggies at your party.

http://easyweb.easynet.co.uk/~monte/index.html

The International Sinatra Society

This shrine to the "Chairman of the Board" has pages on Frank Sinatra's music and movies, as well as posters, videos, books, and magazine articles on or about the performer.

http://www.sinatraclub.com

Leisure Lab

This site is dedicated to cocktail music. Okay, I run the record label. Still, you'll find lots of great stuff, including links to related sites.

http://www.leisurelab.com

Kovacksland Online

This site is dedicated to Ernie Kovacs, one of the most unique talents on early television and a film star. He died in a car crash in the 1960s. Kovacs' wit made him a hit with the party crowd during the heydays of the cocktail party, the 1950s.

```
http://www.users.interport.net/~manaben/
Kparent.html
```

The Rat Pack Homepage

Travel to the home page of this site and you'll get to see a picture of the Rat Pack — partying and performing actors Frank Sinatra, Dean Martin, Sammy Davis, Jr., Peter Lawford, and Joey Bishop — in front of the marquee at Las Vegas' legendary Sands Hotel. Click on a couple of the linked pages and you can see all kinds of pages on the Pack, even — sniff! — a little film of the Sands being demolished to clear the way for a new hotel.

```
http://www.primenet.com/~drbmbay/index.html
```

The Roots of Lounge

The self-proclaimed "Home for Hepcats" — especially the Lounge/Not Lounge section, "The Aesthetic."

```
http://www.gonix.com:80/rol/
```

Space Age Bachelor Pad Music

Not only will you find some great reading on the space age bachelor pad movement and key musicians, but you can download music samples and view the Gallery of Exotic Album Covers.

```
http://www.chaoskitty.com/sabpm/index.html
```

Swank-O-Rama: The Cocktail Revolution Homepage

"Dedicated to better living through Cocktail Culture," this site features not only music and drink recipes, it also features diagrams on some of the classic cocktail party dance steps.

http://www.cyborganic.com/People/jpmckay/

Vik Trola's Lounge of Self-Indulgence

This site features linked pages that share drink and hors d'oeuvre recipes (try the Swedish meatballs!) and music samples.

http://www.chaoskitty.com/t_chaos/lounge.html

Chapter 14

Ten-Plus Films to Inspire Cocktail Consumption

. . . .

*H*ollywood has long been enamored with the cocktail. Cocktails can be found in films featuring everyone from Fred Astaire and James Bond to the Muppets (yes, the Muppets).

But when choosing movies either to show at a party or to get into the cocktail mood, remember this: Just because a film has a scene with a cocktail party doesn't automatically mean you should consider the movie a great cocktail epic. I rate films on what I call *cocktailability* — how well it portrays the lounge lifestyle. Rather than the four stars that movie critics often give out, I give top cocktail movies four martinis.

This chapter includes some of the best cocktail movies of all time, along with their cocktailability rating. Let me point out that a good cocktailability score doesn't mean the film got good reviews from critics. Many a rotten movie has scored high in cocktailability. And some of the best cocktail films don't have much cocktail action, but they do have cocktail quality.

The Bond Films

Unquestionably, the James Bond films have done more for the cocktail movement in the past 35 years than all of the other films combined. The debonair British secret agent's "shaken, not stirred" vodka martini became as well known among the partying public as it did with his adversaries.

But which Bond film is the best? I think every actor who played Bond was excellent, so I've tried to select films giving an example of each actor's "cocktailability quotient."

Dr. No (1962). Bond: Sean Connery.

The first Bond film was one of the coolest. From the moment Connery says, "My name is Bond, James Bond," you knew there were sequels to come!

Cocktails also played a prominent role. In an early scene Bond is brought a medium-dry vodka martini by a waiter who says, "Mixed like you said, sir, and not stirred." Later, Bond pours himself a Smirnoff on the rocks, smells it, and puts it back. Then he takes a bottle of Black Label Smirnoff out of his bag and pours that instead. Was his drink poisoned, or did he decide to go for the premium brand out of personal taste?

Casino Royale (1967). Bond: David Niven.

The only early Bond film not made by British producer Albert Broccoli, *Casino Royale* was actually made as something of a spoof on the other Bond films. Champagne is the alcohol of choice, although it's usually poisoned. Niven's Bond renames the entire division after himself; hires Ursula Andress to take Peter Sellers and turn him into a master spy/baccarat player; and is far more eager to solve the mysterious abductions of all the world's other spies with a champagne glass in his hand than with his Walther PPK handgun. Niven wears some stylin' threads, though!

On Her Majesty's Secret Service (1968). Bond: George Lazenby.

This was his only film as 007, but Lazenby proved to be a great Bond, even though this film had a tragic finale (if I told you, it would spoil the surprise).

The intro to the film features a groovy arrangement to the Bond theme song while a British flag is imposed over a martini glass. The only thing slightly un-cocktail is that Lazenby is the only Bond to wear a toque in a ski chase.

The Man with the Golden Gun (1974). Bond: Roger Moore.

This film was Moore's second shot playing Bond, but many find this (and perhaps *The Spy Who Loved Me,* which followed) his very best. Christopher Lee plays the perfect villain, and Herve Villechaize adds some comic relief as his sidekick, Nick Nack. Bond drinks wine, champagne, and vodka martinis; smokes a cigar; and again is surrounded by beautiful women.

My favorite kitsch moment is the car chase, which reminds me of *The Dukes of Hazard* chasing the guys from *Fantasy Island* in the car from *Starsky and Hutch*.

ҰҰҰ **The Living Daylights** (1987). Bond: Timothy Dalton.

The beginning of each Bond movie has our hero drawing his gun, pointing, and firing. Although Dalton's quick draw pose reminds me of Billy the Kid, his gadgets and love of martinis is pure Bond. Being the "politically correct" 1980s, Bond is much less a womanizer. In fact, Bond's boss, M, is a woman in this film.

Nevertheless, Bond's a handsome devil who still manages to get the girl in the end. My favorite line is when a double agent says, "I might as well ask if all the vodka martinis ever silenced all the screams of all the men you killed!" Hmmm . . . never thought of that. I should mention Dalton's next (and last) Bond film was *Licence to Kill*, which features an excellent cameo by the king of Las Vegas, Wayne Newton.

ҰҰҰ **Goldeneye** (1995). Bond: Pierce Brosnan.

This Bond film is the most successful to date, making almost double the money of any other movie in the series. Brosnan is rugged like Connery, suave like Moore, and sensitive like Dalton — an ideal actor for the role! For my taste, the script is still a little too politically correct, but cool stunts put it at the top of my list. One cocktail note: As vodka martinis have become accepted around the world, Bond's usual vodka, Red Label Smirnoff, changed to the more expensive (and harder to find) Smirnoff Black Label.

Other Great Cocktail Spies

I don't know why, but spies and cocktails seem to go together well on the silver screen. Here are a few other notable espionage efforts that rate highly for cocktailability.

ҰҰҰҰ **The Silencers** (1966). Dean Martin as Matt Helm.

Dino makes an amazing secret agent, but how much can one spy drink? This is the first of four Helm flicks Martin made; it is usually considered his best. Stella Stevens is terrific in the lead female role. The other films are all worth seeing, and include *Murderers' Row, The*

Ambushers, and *The Wrecking Crew.* After that, Martin did a made-for-TV movie and a brief television series, titled *Matt Helm,* in 1975.

 Our Man Flint (1966). James Coburn as Derek Flint.

Another Bond spoof, but one that stands on its own merit. Coburn is so hip it hurts, and Flint's amazing home may give you interior decorating ideas! This cool flick was followed by a sequel, *In Like Flint,* and a made-for-TV movie. Although not playing Flint, Coburn also played the man from Z.O.W.I.E. in *The President's Analyst,* a film too good not to mention somewhere.

 Austin Powers: International Man of Mystery (1997). Mike Myers as Austin Powers.

Myers had a lot of inspiration to draw from in this hilarious spy comedy. Bits of Bond, a dash of Flint, and a pinch of Helm can be found throughout the film, along with some way-out fashion. The great soundtrack includes Burt Bacharach and Brazil 66.

The movie received enough great reviews and money from the box office to make a sequel almost a shoo-in. I just hope that Powers' arch enemy, Dr. Evil, comes back for more.

 Modesty Blaise (1966). Monica Vitti as Modesty Blaise.

Flint, Helm, and Blaise were released all in the same year. Bizzaro! This film has a British artsy feel, but also seems more like a spoof than your average Bond flick. Co-stars Terrence Stamp and Dirk Bogard look mighty young in this one. Modesty may be the perfect role model for the hostess of a spy theme party.

The Rat Pack

Hollywood's Rat Pack (Frank Sinatra, Dean Martin, Sammy Davis, Jr., Joey Bishop, and Peter Lawford) partied and performed during the late 1950s and early 1960s. When they weren't in Las Vegas, where they would often have a few cocktails on stage, they were out shooting a picture, where they loved to drink on the set. If a scene involved drinking, then they'd often shoot the scene repeatedly — for the sake of continuity, of course. Ergo, Rat Pack movies usually have at least one really good cocktail scene.

Here are a few of the Rat Pack's best efforts:

 Ocean's Eleven (1960). Quintissential caper movie with the Rat Pack hoi palloi. Arguably the Chairman and the boys at their finest.

Robin and the Seven Hoods (1964). The Rat Pack go gangster in a Prohibition period re-working of Robin Hood. Look for Sammy's wonderful ode to the joys of emptying a machine gun in the video version, cut out of most TV broadcasts.

Salt and Pepper (1968). Lawford and Davis run a swank London Night Club and run afoul of the local gangsters and the constabulary. Much Clouseau-style comedy follows.

 By the way, check out Chapter 13 for the Web address for the Unofficial Rat Pack Homepage. For an unofficial *Ocean's Eleven* tribute Web page, try http://www.users.interport.net/~timmu/.

The Elegance of Fred Astaire

Whether dancing cheek to cheek with Ginger Rogers, makin' like a Beatnik with Audrey Hepburn, or waltzing across the ceiling, Fred Astaire was off the cocktailability scale. Here are a few of his best cocktail efforts:

 Funny Face (1957). Astaire plays a fashion photographer who makes Audrey Hepburn a famous model. The movie features cocktail classics such as "How Long Has This Been Going On" and "S'Wonderful."

Top Hat (1935). Probably the best film Astaire made with Ginger Rogers. Featuring a cameo by Lucille Ball and songs by Irving Berlin, including "Cheek to Cheek."

Royal Wedding (1950). Astaire dances on the ceiling and sings a duet with Jane Powell called "How Could You Believe Me When I Said I Loved You (When You Know I've Been a Liar All My Life?)" in this classic.

Swing Time (1936). Another one of Fred's finest, *Swing Time* features songs written by Jerome Kern and Dorothy Fields, including "A Fine Romance," "Pick Yourself Up," and "The Way You Look Tonight."

Follow the Fleet (1936). Another Lucille Ball appearance, and some Berlin tunes: "Let's Face the Music and Dance" and "Let Yourself Go." Although Astaire is usually in a tuxedo, he looks surprising comfortable as a sailor.

The Appeal of Mae West

Mae West had an awareness of style and cocktail cool that is to most of our feeble efforts as the Mayan calendar is to a digital watch. West single-handedly saved Paramount Studios, when the folks there realized just how well sex sells tickets. Some of her best efforts include:

I'm No Angel (1933). Mae finds, follows, then and tries to win society pretty-boy Cary Grant. Beulah, peel this woman a grape!

She Done Him Wrong (1933). Mae outlines pre-cocktail languor as Bowery bar owner Lady Lou in her best flick. The film was banned in Austria after opening night in 1933.

Goin To Town (1935). Mae crashes society functions, forcing patrons and matrons alike to splutter and gag on their vermouth.

Myra Breckinridge (1970). Mae keeps a garden of pretty boys and sets an example for post-sex change Raquel Welch.

Sextette (1978). She was old, and was fastened to a plank under her dress and carted on wheels from set to set, but Mae wasn't going to give up the cocktail ghost until she was good and ready. Watch as she marries a prince (played by a pre-Bond Timothy Dalton) in a cocktail-ish flick so self-forgivingly excessive it rivals Russ Meyer films.

Some Efforts Worth Cheers-ing

Not every great cocktail party movie is based on a character, actor or actress, or genre. Consider these fine films:

The Thin Man (1934). Learn the REAL rhythm to mix Manhattans and martinis to. Chuckle as Nick (William Powell) and Nora (Myrna Loy) nurse hangovers. See the archetypical 1930s Christmas party. Watch cocktail after cocktail go down. This film is something of a novelty — a great film as well as a terrific cocktail movie.

Breakfast at Tiffany's (1961). Realizing the essential dream of every small-town Lulla-Mae to become a sophisticated Holly Golightly, even if it means nothing more than lonely breakfasts and window shopping at Tiffany's, Audrey Hepbourn shines in this bittersweet comedy that sets a cocktail standard that is still hard to match. I suspect that if this film were remade today, Patricia Neal's part as George Peppard's "sugar mama" would be played by a man.

The Party (1968). Peter Sellers plays a bumbling Indian actor accidentally invited to a cocktail party, where he trashes a bathroom, learns to shoot pool, and saves Claudine Longet from the machinations of an evil pre-*Love Boat* Gavin MacLeod. You'll think you have seen everything possible at a cocktail party, and then they start scrubbing an elephant in the swimming pool . . . a must see!

All About Eve (1950). A tour de force cocktail bitch performance by Bette Davis sets the mood in this terrific picture about back-biting and politics in the 1940s New York theater scene. George Saunders and Anne Baxter tip the balance in the "Qu'en Mas Cocktail" sweepstakes in this one.

Beyond The Valley of The Dolls (1970). As his psyche-delic cocktail party rises to a fever pitch, boy rock genius-entrepreneur Ronnie "Z-Man" Bartell screams, "This is my happening, and it freaks me out!" The scene, complete with Strawberry Alarm Clock playing in the background, was repeated in *Austin Powers.*

This film has the most unusual cocktail party guests I've ever seen. It's closer to Felini's *Satyricon* than any Bond film. Plenty of hippy jargon and great outfits.

You can find a related Web page at: http://sashimi.wwa.com/~jjf/.

Barbarella (1968). The op-art-iest of '60s op-art science fiction finds Jane Fonda (before Ted Turner paid to have her de-programmed) as a bubble-breasted heroine joined by a half-naked Angel as they search the pleasure dens of the most evil planet in the universe.

You can find an unofficial *Barbarella* Web page at: `http://www.xnet.com/~navta/Barbarella/barb.html`.

Danger: Diabolik (1967). Funny how Batman, Phantom, and Spawn of the 1990s still can't hold a candle to this suave '60s dude in lycra. A combination spy/caper film from many of the same people who would go on to do *Barbarella*, this psychedelic movie stars John Philip Law as the cool, leather-clad title villain and Marisa Mell as his accomplice. Incredible outré sets, sexy costumes and one of Ennio Morricone's grooviest soundtracks. While there isn't a cocktail party in sight, the movie is guaranteed to get you in the mood to buy some new clothes or revamp your living room.

Sweet Charity (1969). Sammy Davis, Jr. plays a cuddly Mansonesque cult leader-gone lounge guru known as "Daddy" who preaches the rhythm of life to Shirley MacLaine and her boyfriend on their first date. The ULTRA perfect lounge, the Pompei Club, is where Ricardo Montalban takes sweet little urchin MacLaine. Look for high-jumping Ben Vereen in a fabulous freak-out dance sequence that looks like what Rowen & Martin's *Laugh-In* might have been if it was a Gene Kelly production number.

The Love God? (1969). Who can resist Don Knotts in any film? He's better known as Barney Fife on *The Andy Griffith Show*, or Mr. Furley on *Three's Company*, or even as a fish in *The Incredible Mr. Limpett*, but *The Love God?* contains his highest cocktailability factor. In this film, a publishing company sets Knotts up as their patsy by making him into the next Hugh Hefner. Kind of Walter Mitty goes cocktail by way of Mr. Chicken.

Chapter 15

Ten Cocktail Heroes

In This Chapter

▶ Milton Berle

▶ James Bond

▶ Sammy Davis, Jr.

▶ Hugh Hefner

▶ John F. Kennedy

▶ Jerry Lewis

▶ Dean Martin

▶ Dorothy Parker

▶ Cole Porter

▶ Frank Sinatra

*F*inesse. Pizzazz. Elegance. Some men and women fairly scream "cocktail." And the true cocktail aficionado croons to be like them. The people profiled in this chapter are Catholic and Jewish, black and white, fictitious and real, but they all have that smooth, suave demeanor that makes you want to settle into a tuxedo and puff on a cigar if you're a man or slip into an elegant dress and carry a cigarette holder if you're a woman. These people are cocktail heroes.

Milton Berle

If Milton Berle, born July 12, 1908 in New York City, had only been known for dressing in drag, smoking a cigar, introducing America to Elvis Presley, or appearing as "Louie the Lilac" on the campy '60s *Batman* television series, he would have earned a place in the Cocktail Hall of Fame.

But Berle, who was fifty years old when the *Milton Berle Show* premiered in 1958, was also a pioneer of the television medium. Thus he earned the nickname "Mr. Television" in addition to being "Uncle Miltie" to millions of people in the postwar suburban affluence that was the fifties and sixties.

Like all good heroes of the cocktail cause, Berle appeared in two of the best "heist" movies of the sixties, 1963's *It's a Mad Mad Mad Mad World* and 1967's money-printing fantasy, *Who's Minding the Mint?* That too, would be enough to grant him hall-of-famer status.

But Milton Berle, whose career started in vaudeville before hits on Broadway, radio, movies, and television, really cinched his spot in the hall of fame in 1997 with the publication of *MILTON* magazine.

The magazine, dedicated to the person who "works hard and plays hard, enjoying the finest things life has to offer, striving for success while making time to party," is essentially a gaming guide for the Las Vegas crowd. This publication is unafraid in these politically correct times to bear the motto: "We Drink, We Smoke, We Gamble."

In its premiere issue, *MILTON* magazine features included: "Playing Blackjack without Looking Like a Dork," "Rating the Top 5 Rums and Tequilas," "The 10 Premium Cigars," and a piece called "Hollywood Invades Las Vegas." Way to go, Uncle Miltie!

James Bond

Ian Fleming's fictional creation of secret agent 007, James Bond, is considered the template for all groovy cool secret agents. Originally portrayed in films by a young, suave Sean Connery in *Dr. No* (1962), *From Russia with Love* (1963), *Goldfinger* (1964), *Thunderball* (1965), and *You Only Live Twice* (1967), Bond is the archetype of the gun-toting, woman-loving, martini-sipping man of the world. The very name — Bond — suggests sound currency, good vodka, and integrity.

Like the heroes of classical myth, Bond is at home on land, sea, and air. In any crisis he knows just what to do and how to handle himself. And, of course, he's always surrounded by some of the most beautiful women in the world.

Besides Sean Connery, who many consider the quintessential Bond, Roger Moore is also very much the Bond type. And give credit to George Lazenby, who only made one Bond movie *(On Her Majesty's Secret Service)* before being re-placed by Moore. After Timothy Dalton's brief reign in the '80s, Pierce Brosnan has finally returned James Bond to the pantheon of cool a whole 35 years after Connery's first utterance of the phrase, "My name is Bond. James Bond."

Sammy Davis, Jr.

NEVER DUG YOU BEFORE. DUG YOU LAST NIGHT. YOU THE MAN. MARLON.

— telegram to Sammy Davis, Jr. from Marlon Brando, January 12, 1955.

Born on December 8, 1925, in Harlem, Sammy Davis, Jr. died on May 16, 1990, in Beverly Hills. The only man of color in Sinatra's Rat Pack, Davis' spiritual home was represented by the glitter and glamour of Las Vegas.

Overlooked by Oscar, snubbed by the Grammy, Tony-less, and ignored by the Emmy, Sammy Davis, Jr. was nonetheless the dictionary definition of the word *entertainer*.

Shortly after a car accident in which he lost his eye, Sammy converted to Judaism. That said, his notoriety as the only cycloptic black Jew in the Rat Pack was the source of much of his funniest material. His combination of hep cat swingin' jazz lingo and stone-faced religious fervor was perhaps most evident in his speech from the Shirley MacClaine film *Sweet Charity:*

1. Thou shalt dig thy neighbor as thou wouldst have thy neighbor dig thee.
2. Thou shalt not put down thy mamas and thy papas.
3. Thou shalt not swing with another cat's chick.
4. Thou shalt not blow thy mind on school nights and national holidays.

Of his devotion to show biz, Davis once summed up: "A variety artist, that's what I am. You can't please everybody. But you please the majority and don't ever let them say,

'Gee, I didn't like the performance.' That doesn't mean everybody is going to like what you're doing, but at least they can say, 'He performed for me, man. He gave his all.'"

His hit version of the song "Candy Man" still stands as a beacon of Vegas showbiz glitz. And speaking of card games, in the bigoted words of Archie Bunker from the now legendary "Sammy's Visit" episode of *All in the Family,* Sammy Davis, Jr. was, and I quote, "the ace of spades." Read his autobiography, *Yes, I Can: The Story of Sammy Davis, Jr.* (Noonday Press), and you'll agree that he was one of the most talented and hardest-working entertainers of all time.

Hugh Hefner

The controversial founder and bunny master of *Playboy* magazine will forever live as a symbol of man's desire for pleasure and leisure.

Hugh M. Hefner has enraged feminists as much as he has entertained the male population with his bachelor-centric magazine that was audacious enough to include color nude centerfolds amongst other adult interests like jazz reviews, original fiction by bestselling authors, and martini recipes.

Before "Hef" launched the magazine, there really wasn't a definitive expression of the leisure life in America. Always the softest of the nudie magazines, *Playboy* was and still is a style guide for the single man who likes the finer things in life. Political incorrectness aside, his unflinching pursuit of hedonism alone earns him a place in the Cocktail Hall of Fame.

The image of Hefner in his red velvet robe, pipe in hand, with several scantily clad "bunnies" became the unspoken ideal of the swinging young man of the '60s. During a time when the sexual revolution was raging nonstop, Hef was its Che Guevara, fighting for freedom of speech in the cocktail-soaked trenches of his many Playboy Mansions.

His *Playboy after Dark* television program helped redefine late-night TV in the pre-Letterman '70s. While Bob Guccione and Larry Flynt both imitated the form, both failed to emulate the real secret of *Playboy:* that true freedom is based on a sense of style, not just some staples in a naked model's midriff.

John F. Kennedy

Ich Bin Ein Berliner was his famous quote, but *Ich Bin Ein Swinger* may have been more of a suitable quote for U.S. President John Fitzgerald Kennedy. With his sexy wife, Jacqueline, the two were the epitome of modness.

Here was a man with power, good looks, and his own private party plane, Air Force One! Having proved his coolness quip-for-quip in a televised debate flattening then-Senator Richard Nixon, America fell in love with this stylish ladies' man.

Jackie's dress sense and JFK's buttoned-down sense of style made them a hit as far away as the streets of Paris. On one official French visit, Jackie caused such a stir with the fashion-conscious Francophones that Kennedy remarked that he felt like he was escorting Mrs. Kennedy rather than the other way around.

The fact that Kennedy was pals with both Jerry Lewis and Frank Sinatra, not to mention his alleged flings with iconic movie star Marilyn Monroe, only fortify his stature as a man who understood party politics, Democrat and Republican alike. The politics of the party were JFK's stock and trade. Sadly, his assassination in 1963 also killed the party.

Jerry Lewis

Ask a Frenchman from the golden era of French New Wave Cinema about Jerry Lewis and the word *auteur* will follow. Besides being a renowned genius in the world of film, Lewis is also a true cocktail hero.

His work as the goofy one in the comedy team of Martin and Lewis ensures him an honorable mention, and his association with JFK brings him closer to Cocktail Hall of Fame status. But for many, it is his portrayal of the Über lounge lizard Buddy Love in the film *The Nutty Professor* that cinches his entry in the annals of chic.

Buddy is the impulsive and brash, but always cool and slicked-back, creation of Lewis' alter ego. The first arrival of Buddy Love in the cocktail bar scene is a priceless gem of cocktailia. Add to this the fact that Lewis was the progenitor of that most sweaty and cheesy of genres, the telethon.

While obviously for a great cause, the Muscular Dystrophy Association, these enduro shows were the beginning and end of America's schmaltz era.

Suitably, the MDA telethons are held in that land of glitz and exotica, Las Vegas, and frequently have drop-in appearances by all or some of the Rat Pack and such entertainers as Susan Anton, Joey Heatherton, and Liza Minneli. At the time of this writing, Lewis is touring North America in the musical *Damn Yankees,* in which he wears stunning loungewear. Cheers.

Dean Martin

Dean Martin was the clown prince of the Rat Pack. Renowned for his smooth singing voice, his alcohumor ("Boy, I was so loaded last night that when I fell down, I missed the floor"), and, of course, Matt Helm movies.

In the '40s and '50s, "Dino" got his first taste of fame (and no doubt bourbon) in a duo with Jerry Lewis, and then broke out on his own in movies and TV. Later he went on to the highest level of showbiz royalty — he was considered "a brother" by the "Chairman of the Board," Frank Sinatra.

Born Dino Paul Crocetti on June 7, 1917, in Steubenville, Ohio, the son of Italian immigrants dropped out of school at 16 to become a croupier in a backroom club called the Rex. His rise as a smooth-voiced sex symbol for the emerging suburban middle class of the '50s and '60s led one unknown pundit to opine, "What Andy Warhol was to the hip New York art and fashion world, Dean Martin was to rootless, suburban Middle America."

When his hit "Everybody Loves Somebody" robbed the Beatles of their No. 1 slot in 1964, it was proof to the world that Dino was here to stay. His NBC variety show, featuring the sexy Gold Diggers dance troupe, was so popular that admirers such as Elvis Presley publicly envied Martin's staying power.

Although he made some serious stabs at drama in films like *Rio Bravo* and *Some Came Running*, it will always be the Matt Helm pictures, in the tail end of the swingin' sixties, that earn him a place in the Cocktail Hall of Fame. Those Bond-like spoofs, now available on video, were *The Silencers*

(1966), *Murderer's Row* (1966), *The Ambushers* (1968), and *The Wrecking Crew* (1969). Dean Martin died of emphysema on Christmas Day, 1995.

Dorothy Parker

An American critic, satirical poet, and short-story writer, Dorothy Rothschild Parker is probably better remembered for her caustic one-liners than for her poetry and stories.

Born in West End, New Jersey, on August 22, 1893, Parker got her start by selling some poetry to *Vogue* magazine. That led to a position with the magazine, which led to a position as drama critic of *Vanity Fair*; she eventually was a contributor to and a major force in shaping *The New Yorker*. Parker's precise, epigrammatic style rivaled Oscar Wilde's, maybe even F. Scott Fitzgerald's, and was perfect for capturing the voice of the Roaring Twenties. Later on she worked for Hollywood, where her film credits included *A Star is Born* and *Saboteur*.

Parker was also the grand dame of the Algonquin Hotel's famed Round Table (the core group of cocktail intelligentsia in New York in the 1920s). She may have been gloomy, but she put words together with the finesse of a master barkeep mixing a Manhattan. Some choice Parker bits:

- ✔ "Brevity is the soul of lingerie."
- ✔ "Men seldom make passes at girls who wear glasses."
- ✔ "Look at him, a rhinestone in the rough."
- ✔ "You know, that woman speaks 18 languages, and she can't say 'no' in any of them."
- ✔ In a book review: "This is not a novel to be tossed aside lightly. It should be thrown aside with great force."
- ✔ In a play review, about Katharine Hepburn's acting ability: "Miss Hepburn runs the gamut of emotions from A to B." (By the way, I don't agree. I like Hepburn.)
- ✔ When told that U.S. President Calvin Coolidge had died: "How can they tell?"
- ✔ Parker died on June 7, 1967. Her choice for her epitaph: "Excuse my dust."

An unofficial Dorothy Parker Web site: http://www.users.interport.net/~lynda/dorothy.html.

Cole Porter

Cole Porter was a celebrated singer and bon vivant. His wealthy parents doted on him. Considered a "mama's boy" in school, he made friends by writing satirical songs about his teachers. He wrote musicals even while attending Yale University and Harvard Law School. His first major hit was "Let's Do It" in 1928; "Anything Goes" in 1930 cemented his popularity.

Although heir to a fortune, he married Linda Thomas, a society child who was more wealthy than Porter's family. Porter was a homosexual, but his wife was happy to act as a Den Mother for her husband's entourage as well as something of a personal supporter or manager.

Porter counted cocktail aficionados Ernest Hemingway and F. Scott Fitzgerald among his friends. Not only are Porter's songs among the most popular at cocktail parties today, but his Opening Night parties were also legendary. He threw wild bashes at his place in Venice, and did much to popularize the French Riviera amongst those Americans discovering Europe for the first time.

Frank Sinatra

The "Chairman Of The Board." "The Voice." "Ol' Blue Eyes." Francis Albert Sinatra has garnered more nicknames than you have hot dinners, baby!

Born December 12, 1915, in Hoboken, New Jersey, young Frank grew up idolizing Bing Crosby and fantasizing about being a singer. By 1939, after a short stint in Harry James' big band and, more importantly, as Tommy Dorsey's "boy singer," Frank was not only a renowned vocalist but a major teen idol, earning the moniker "The Voice That Thrilled Millions" (later shortened to "The Voice").

Sinatra's classic recordings for Columbia and later recordings for Capitol are ample evidence that the cat could swing. An excellent documentary on his life, "The House I Live In," was released in 1945. Despite alleged links to organized crime and alleged Communist sympathies that led to an appearance before the Committee on Un-American Activities,

Sinatra's charisma was such that his popularity could never be diminished, despite gossip that his career was on the decline.

By accepting a huge fee cut to star in *From Here To Eternity* (1953), Sinatra not only won an Oscar for Best Supporting Actor, but managed to orchestrate a comeback that proved once and for all that he wasn't going to Palookaville without a fight. The year 1955 saw him star in three classic Sinatra films: *The Tender Trap, Guys and Dolls,* and *The Man with the Golden Arm.* In 1956, Sinatra made *Meet Me in Las Vegas* for MGM. Many other films — like *The Manchurian Candidate* (1962) and *Tony Rome* (1967) — cemented his cinematic reputation.

By this time, Sinatra had taken over the reins of the Rat Pack (a group of hard-partying men from the entertainment world) from Humphrey Bogart. It was in *Ocean's Eleven* (1960) where Frank, as smooth-talking Danny Ocean, really made a statement that some consider the manifesto of the Rat Pack. The Rat Pack made films together (including 1964's *Robin and the Seven Hoods,* which Sinatra produced), sang together, and even toured together.

Sinatra has been married to Ava Gardner and Mia Farrow and linked to Lauren Bacall and Juliet Prowse, among others. He reportedly dislikes women who smoke, drink too much, or who wear heavy perfume. Although he has gone on record as saying that Jack Daniels is his favorite alcoholic beverage, actress Rosalind Russell once called Ol' Blue Eyes "a fake drinker . . . more often than not, he talks more about drinking than he actually imbibes."

In addition to 49 Grammy awards, Sinatra has had 21 gold albums and received platinum albums for "Strangers In The Night" in 1966 and "Greatest Hits" in 1968. Sinatra's all-star vocal collection, "Duets," (1994) won the crooner his first multi-platinum record from the Recording Industry Association of America for two million units sold.

Cocktail Discography

· ·

*Y*ou know that a party isn't really swinging if it's Tony Bennettless. You've read Chapter 7 and the suggestions I have there, but what other musicians go over well at a cocktail party? A complete listing of all of the cocktail party music in the world would be enormous, but to help you out, I've put together this list, which contains some of my favorite re-issues and some of the better-known modern groups doing cocktail music.

The list is grouped by artist or group and includes the record labels for each record. I have not included all the easy listening or big band records by legends like Bennett, Frank Sinatra, Sammy Davis, Jr., Mel Torme, Peggy Lee, Ella Fitzgerald, Dean Martin, and so on; you already know those people are happening!

Maya Angelou

Miss Calypso — Scamp

Les Baxter

Colors of Brazil/African Blue — GNP Crescendo

Les Baxter's Best — Capitol/EMI

Que Mango — Scamp

The Exotic Moods of Les Baxter — Capitol/EMI

The Lost Episode — Bacchus Archives

Jaymz Bee and The Royal Jelly Orchestra

ClintEastWoodyAllenAlda — Leisure Lab/BMG Canada

A Christmas Cocktail — Milan/BMG

Cocktail: Shaken and Stirred — Milan /BMG

Frank Bennett

Five O'Clock Shadow — Mercury /Polydor

James Bond and His Sextet

Plays the James Bond Songbook — Rykodisc

Jack "Bongo" Burger

The End on Bongos — Rykodisc

Combustible Edison

I, Swinger — SubPop

Schizophonic! — SubPop

Martin Denny

Afro-Desia — Scamp

Exotica 1 & Exotica 2 — Scamp

Forbidden Island & Primitiva — Scamp

Exotica — The Best of Martin Denny — Rhino

The Exotic Sounds of Martin Denny — Rhino

Enoch Light

Music Maestro, Please — Project 3 (cassette only)

Persuasive Percussion — Varese Vintage

Spanish Strings — Project 3

Provocative Percussion — Varese Vintage

Juan Esquivel

Space-Age Bachelor Pad Music — Bar None

Music from a Sparkling Planet — Bar None

Merry Xmas from the Space-Age Bachelor Pad — Bar None

Cabaret Mañana — RCA/BMG

More of Other Worlds, Other Sounds — Warner Archives

101 Strings

Astro Sounds from Beyond the Year 2000 — Scamp

Dick Hyman

Moog: The Electric Eclectics of Dick Hyman — UNI/Varese Sarabande

The In Group

New Sounds — The Swinging 12 String Guitar — Rykodisc

Antonio Carlos Jobim

The Man From Ipanema (box) — Verve

The Composer Plays — Verve

The Art of Antonio Carlos Jobim — Verve

The Wonderful World of Antonio Carlos Jobim — Discovery

Urubu — Warner Archives

Some of The Best — Laserlight

Personalidade (Best of Brazil) — Verve

Arthur Lyman

Taboo — Rykodisc

Taboo Vol. 2 — Rykodisc

Aphrodisia — Rykodisc

Henry Mancini

The Best of Mancini — RCA

The Pink Panther, Baby Elephant Walk — RCA

The Second Time Around . . . and Others — RCA

Moon River — RCA

Peter Gunn — Laserlight

Pure Gold — RCA

Robert Mitchum

Calypso Is Like So. . . — Scamp

Hugo Montenegro

The Good, the Bad and the Ugly — RCA

Overture American Music Theatre, Volumes 1–4 — Bainbridge

Montenegro Plays the Movies — Bainbridge

Pizzicato Five

Made in USA — Matador

The Sound of Music by Pizzicato Five — Matador

Combinaison Spaciale EP — Matador

Magic Carpet Ride EP — Matador

Five By Five EP — Matador

Happy Sad (maxi single) — Matador

Squirrel Nut Zippers

Hot — Mammoth

The Inevitable — Mammoth

Tim Tamashiro

Wise-Ass Crooner — BMG/Leisure Lab

Ultra-Lounge Series (Various Artists)

Volume 1: Mondo Exotica — Capitol/EMI

Volume 2: Mambo Fever — Capitol/EMI

Volume 3: Space Capades — Capitol/EMI

Volume 4: Bachelor Pad Royale — Capitol/EMI

Volume 5: Wild Cool and Swingin' — Capitol/EMI

Volume 6: Rhapsodesia — Capitol/EMI

Volume 7: The Crime Scene — Capitol/EMI

Volume 8: Cocktail Capers — Capitol/EMI

Volume 9: Cha Cha De Amor — Capitol/EMI

Volume 10: A Bachelor in Paradise — Capitol/EMI

Volume 11: Organs in Orbit — Capitol/EMI

Volume 12: Saxophobia — Capitol/EMI

Volume 13: TV Town — Capitol/EMI

Volume 14: Bossa Novaville — Capitol/EMI

Volume 15: Wild, Cool & Swingin' Too! — Capitol/EMI

Volume 16: Mondo Hollywood — Capitol/EMI

Volume 17: Bongoland — Capitol/EMI

Volume 18: Bottoms Up — Capitol/EMI

Ultra-Lounge Christmas Cocktails — Capitol/EMI

Ultra-Lounge Leopard-Skin Sampler — Capitol/EMI

Walter Wanderley

Samba Swing — Scamp

Harry Zimmerman Big Band

Bongos/Reeds/Brass, Vol. 2 — Rykodisc

Various Artists

Another Crazy Cocktail Party/Shake Your Congas — RCA/BMG

The Love Handle Lounge — Laserlight

Lounge Music Goes Latin — Polygram/Chronicles

Exotic Embers, Forgotten Moons — Laserlight (Stanyan)

Hip-O Cigar Classics — Hip-O

Lounge Legends — K-tel

Cocktail Mix Vol. 4 — Soundtracks with a Twist — Rhino

Safe Sax — Laserlight

How Big Is Your Woofer? — Laserlight

HiFi Records' *Living Presence* series (distributed by Rykodisc)

Bob Florence: Bongos/Reeds/Brass — Rykodisc

The Sound Gallery, Volume 1 — Scamp

The Sound Gallery, Volume 2 — EMI/Premier

Tipsy: *Trip Tease* — Asphodel

Index

IDG BOOKS WORLDWIDE REGISTRATION CARD

Visit our Web site at
http://www.idgbooks.com

ISBN Number: 0-7645-5026-8

Title of this book: Cocktail Parties For Dummies™

My overall rating of this book: ❑ Very good [1] ❑ Good [2] ❑ Satisfactory [3] ❑ Fair [4] ❑ Poor [5]

How I first heard about this book:

❑ Found in bookstore; name: [6]

❑ Book review: [7]

❑ Advertisement: [8]

❑ Catalog: [9]

❑ Word of mouth; heard about book from friend, co-worker, etc.: [10]

❑ Other: [11]

IDG
BOOKS
WORLDWIDE
THE WORLD OF
COMPUTER
KNOWLEDGE®

What I liked most about this book:

What I would change, add, delete, etc., in future editions of this book:

Other comments:

Number of computer books I purchase in a year: ❑ 1 [12] ❑ 2-5 [13] ❑ 6-10 [14] ❑ More than 10 [15]

I would characterize my computer skills as: ❑ Beginner [16] ❑ Intermediate [17] ❑ Advanced [18] ❑ Professional [19]

I use ❑ DOS [20] ❑ Windows [21] ❑ OS/2 [22] ❑ Unix [23] ❑ Macintosh [24] ❑ Other: [25]_____ (please specify)

I would be interested in new books on the following subjects:

(please check all that apply, and use the spaces provided to identify specific software)

❑ Word processing: [26]   ❑ Spreadsheets: [27]

❑ Data bases: [28]   ❑ Desktop publishing: [29]

❑ File Utilities: [30]   ❑ Money management: [31]

❑ Networking: [32]   ❑ Programming languages: [33]

❑ Other: [34]

I use a PC at (please check all that apply): ❑ home [35] ❑ work [36] ❑ school [37] ❑ other: [38] _____

The disks I prefer to use are ❑ 5.25 [39] ❑ 3.5 [40] ❑ other: [41]_____

I have a CD ROM: ❑ yes [42] ❑ no [43]

I plan to buy or upgrade computer hardware this year: ❑ yes [44] ❑ no [45]

I plan to buy or upgrade computer software this year: ❑ yes [46] ❑ no [47]

Name: _____ Business title: [48] _____

Type of Business: [49]

Address (❑ home [50] ❑ work [51]/Company name: _____

Street/Suite#

City [52]/State [53]/Zip code [54]: _____ Country [55]

❑ **I liked this book!**

You may quote me by name in future IDG Books Worldwide promotional materials.

My daytime phone number is _____

☐ YES!

Please keep me informed about IDG Books Worldwide's World of Computer Knowledge. Send me your latest catalog.

NO POSTAGE
NECESSARY
IF MAILED
IN THE
UNITED STATES

BUSINESS REPLY MAIL

FIRST CLASS MAIL   PERMIT NO. 2605   FOSTER CITY, CALIFORNIA

IDG Books Worldwide
919 E Hillsdale Blvd, Ste 400
Foster City, CA 94404-9691